Customer Relationship Management

Student Manual

THOMSON

COURSE TECHNOLOGY

Australia • Canada • Mexico • Singapore
Spain • United Kingdom • United States

Customer Relationship Management

VP and GM of Courseware:	Michael Springer
Series Product Managers:	Caryl Bahner-Guhin and Adam A. Wilcox
Developmental Editor:	Linda K. Long
Project Editor:	Geraldine Martin
Series Designer:	Adam A. Wilcox
Cover Designer:	Steve Deschene

For more information, go to www.logicaloperations.com

Trademarks

Course ILT is a trademark of Course Technology.

Some of the product names and company names used in this book have been used for identification purposes only and may be trademarks or registered trademarks of their respective manufacturers and sellers.

Disclaimer

Course Technology reserves the right to revise this publication and make changes from time to time in its content without notice.

ISBN 0-619-16141-8

Printed in the United States of America

1 2 3 4 5 PM 06 05 04 03

Contents

Customer Relationship Management

Introduction

After reading this introduction, you will know how to:

A Use Course Technology ILT manuals in general.

B Use prerequisites, a target student description, course objectives, and a skills inventory to properly set your expectations for the course.

Topic A: About the manual

Course Technology ILT philosophy

Course Technology ILT manuals facilitate your learning by providing structured interaction with the subject. While we provide text to explain difficult concepts, the activities are the focus of our courses. By paying close attention as your instructor leads you through these activities, you will learn the concepts effectively.

We believe strongly in the instructor-led classroom. During class, focus on your instructor. Our manuals are designed and written to facilitate your interaction with your instructor, and not to call attention to the manuals themselves.

We believe in the basic approach of setting expectations, delivering instruction, and providing summary and review afterwards. For this reason, lessons begin with objectives and end with summaries. We also provide overall course objectives and a course summary to provide both an introduction to and closure on the entire course.

Manual components

The manuals contain these major components:

- Table of contents
- Introduction
- Units
- Course summary
- Glossary
- Index

Each element is described below.

Table of contents

The table of contents acts as a learning roadmap.

Introduction

The introduction contains information about our training philosophy and our manual components, features, and conventions. It contains descriptions of the target student, objectives, and setup for the course.

Units

Units are the largest structural component of the course content. A unit begins with a title page that lists objectives for each major subdivision, or topic, within the unit. Within each topic, conceptual and explanatory information alternates with activities. Units conclude with a summary comprising one paragraph for each topic, and an independent practice activity that gives you an opportunity to practice the skills you've learned.

The conceptual information takes the form of text paragraphs, exhibits, lists, and tables. The activities contain various types of questions, answers, activities, graphics, and other information.

Course summary

This section provides a text summary of the entire course. It is useful for providing closure at the end of the course. The course summary also indicates the next course in this series, if there is one, and lists additional resources you might find useful as you continue to learn about the subject.

Glossary

The glossary provides definitions for all of the key terms used in this course.

Index

The index enables you to quickly find information about a particular topic or concept of the course.

Manual conventions

We've tried to keep the number of elements and the types of formatting to a minimum in the manuals. This aids in clarity and makes the manuals more classically elegant looking. But there are some conventions and icons you should know about.

Convention	Description
Italic text	In conceptual text, indicates a new term or feature.
Bold text	In unit summaries, indicates a key term or concept. In an independent practice activity, indicates an explicit item that you select, choose, or type.
`Code font`	Indicates code or syntax.

Activities

The activities are the most important parts of our manuals. They are usually divided into two columns, with questions or concepts on the left and answers and explanations on the right. Here's a sample:

Do it!

A-1:   Steps for brainstorming

Exercises

1 Sequence the steps for brainstorming.

Begin generating ideas.

Select the purpose.

Organize for the session.

Ask questions and clarify ideas.

Review the rules.

Topic B: Setting your expectations

Properly setting your expectations is essential to your success. This topic will help you do that by providing:

- A description of the target student at whom the course is aimed
- A list of the objectives for the course
- A skills assessment for the course

Target student

The typical students of this course will be managers, supervisors, or team leaders who need to learn how to manage customers effectively.

Course objectives

These overall course objectives will give you an idea about what to expect from the course. It is also possible that they will help you see that this course is not the right one for you. If you think you either lack the prerequisite knowledge or already know most of the subject matter to be covered, you should let your instructor know that you think you are misplaced in the class.

After completing this course, you will know how to:

- Identify the benefits of loyal customers, create loyal customers, develop customer relationships, and implement the goals of a market intelligent enterprise.
- Identify the goals and types of customer relationship management, and develop a customer relationship management program.
- Manage and reduce costs associated with CRM implementation, and plan a CRM implementation.
- Redesign work processes, identify reasons for implementing CRM in stages, and implement CRM.
- Identify the features and disadvantages of eCRM, and automate CRM through eCRM.
- Customize eCRM and achieve CRM goals through eCRM

Skills inventory

Use the following form to gauge your skill level entering the class. For each skill listed, rate your familiarity from 1 to 5, with five being the most familiar. *This is not a test.* Rather, it is intended to provide you with an idea of where you're starting from at the beginning of class. If you're wholly unfamiliar with all the skills, you might not be ready for the class. If you think you already understand all of the skills, you might need to move on to the next course in the series. In either case, you should let your instructor know as soon as possible.

Skill	1	2	3	4	5
Identifying the benefits of customer loyalty					
Creating loyal customers					
Developing customer relationships					
Implementing MIE goals					
Identifying CRM types					
Identifying CRM goals					
Developing a CRM program					
Managing and reducing costs associated with CRM implementation					
Planning a CRM implementation					
Redesigning work processes					
Identifying reasons to implement CRM in stages					
Implementing CRM					
Identifying eCRM features					
Identifying the disadvantages of eCRM					
Automating CRM through eCRM					
Customizing eCRM					
Achieving CRM goals through eCRM					

Topic C: Reviewing the course

This section explains what you'll need to do in order to be able to review this course after class.

Download the Student Data files for the course:

1. Connect to http://downloads.logicaloperations.com.
2. Enter the course title or search by part to locate this course.
3. Click the course title to display a list of available downloads.
   Note: Data Files are located under the Instructor Edition of the course.
4. Click the link(s) for downloading the Student Data files.
5. Create a folder named Student Data on the desktop of your computer.
6. Double-click the downloaded zip file(s) and drag the contents into the Student Data folder.

Unit 1
Customer loyalty

Unit time: 85 minutes

Complete this unit, and you'll know how to:

A Identify the benefits of loyal customers, and create loyal customers.

B Develop customer relationships, and implement the goals of market intelligent enterprises.

Topic A: Customer loyalty

Explanation

Loyal customers provide profitable contributions to your company. If you can achieve a high level of customer loyalty, then chances are your company will be profitable. Earning customer loyalty involves exceeding their expectations rather than merely satisfying their needs. To achieve customer loyalty, you need to have a long-term commitment to your customers, provide consistently good service, and build relationships with your customers over time. Essentially, the service you provide must make customers want to come back to your company.

Benefits of loyal customers

To create customer loyalty, you need to consider customers as your number one priority. For this, you must plan and implement a long-term service strategy. Your company can experience the following three benefits from customer loyalty.

- Increased spending
- Increased advertising
- Reduced costs

Increased spending

Loyal customers provide profitable contributions to your company because their spending accelerates over time. For example, in the automobile service industry, the average annual revenue per customer triples between the first and fifth year. If you offer a variety of products and services, potential exists for spending growth through cross-selling and up-selling additional products and services. Customers usually purchase more goods and services from you if they are satisfied with their initial purchases.

Increased advertising

Because word-of-mouth advertising accounts for up to 50 percent of the purchases made, your organization must provide a service that customers want to talk about. By simply talking about your service, customers can reduce the amount of money you spend on advertising through media outlets. In addition, this form of advertising is considered more truthful than the advertisements created by the company. It is important to note that customers are more likely to talk about a bad experience than a good one. As a result, providing good service encourages your customers to spread positive messages about your organization.

Reduced costs

Loyal customers can reduce your organizational costs in four ways:

- A loyal customer base greatly reduces the need to acquire new customers because loyal customers are less likely to switch to a competitor.
- Loyal customers might be willing to pay slightly more for your service if they have established a strong relationship with your company.
- Acquiring new customers can cost six times more than maintaining the satisfaction of your current customers.
- Because loyal customers are familiar with your company and the services you offer, they need less assistance from employees.

Do it!   **A-1:   Discussing the benefits of customer loyalty**

Exercises

1 Which of the following are the benefits of creating loyal customers?

   A   Loyal customers increase their spending.

   B   Loyal customers advertise your service.

   C   Loyal customers purchase expensive products.

   D   Loyal customers are innovative.

   E   Loyal customers reduce costs.

   F   Loyal customers don't care if your prices are the lowest.

2 Enact the following role-plays, and discuss the benefits of creating loyal customers.

   In the following scenario, a sales representative is trying to sell a competitor's washing machine to a loyal customer of Icon International.

   Customer: I want to buy an Icon washing machine.

   Sales rep: Why Icon's?

   Customer: I'm using other appliances from Icon and am more than satisfied with their quality and service.

   Sales rep: You know there are other companies offering the same features at a lower cost!

   Customer: Oh, that doesn't matter! I'm ready to spend a little more for the quality and assurance that comes with Icon's products.

   In the following scenario, Pierce is talking to his friend, Gary. During their conversation, they discuss a washing machine that Pierce has recently purchased.

   Gary: What happened to the washing machine that you purchased? You said there was a scratch on it.

   Pierce: Yes there was, but I informed the customer service center of Icon International and they replaced it immediately.

   Gary: Did they charge extra for the service?

   Pierce: Of course not! Because the scratch occurred during transportation, they didn't charge a thing.

   Gary: Wow, that's great. Their service policy is really good, isn't it Pierce?

   Pierce: Of course, it's great! They consider their customers as the top priority and provide only quality products. This is the reason why I've always insisted on buying Icon products.

> In the following scenario, the sales representative is trying to sell a competitor's washing machine to a loyal customer of Icon.
>
> Customer: So, what are you saying?
>
> Sales rep: I'm just asking you to try it. It has many new features, which are not available in the Icon washing machine that you are using!
>
> Customer: I understand that some new features are available in your washing machine. But, I'm just not interested! I feel that my washing machine is best suited to my needs. Besides, I'm personally very impressed by Icon's customer service and have always believed in buying Icon products.
>
> Sales rep: Ok then, if you change your mind, please contact me.
>
> Customer: I don't think I will! However, if I do, I'll contact you. Thanks for your efforts.

Create loyal customers

Explanation

To provide service that exceeds the expectations of customers and brings them back to your organization, you need to do the following:

1 Develop dedicated employees.
2 Make your service memorable.
3 Build relationships with your customers.

Creating dedicated employees

The first step in creating loyal customers is creating dedicated employees. To create dedicated employees, you need to do the following:

- **Make a commitment to employee satisfaction.** By improving employee satisfaction, employee turnover is reduced, so you spend less time training and replacing them.

- **Hire employees with the right skills and attitude for customer service.** If you hire employees who do not like working with people or feel that serving people is beneath them, then you cannot expect to mold them into successful customer service representatives.

- **Provide employee training.** This is critical in developing dedicated employees who can provide high levels of customer service. Every company needs a training plan that teaches new employees the skills that make them competent and empower them to face the challenges of their positions. Training should address new problems as well as changes in the needs of the customers. It should also enable current employees to refresh their skills. Training increases employee commitment to a company because they appreciate this form of support from the management. Training that helps employees sharpen their skills and take on new responsibilities also increases their levels of job satisfaction.

- **Recognize employees for their effort.** Although employees are compensated for their work through wages or salaries, recognizing their efforts is important in terms of job satisfaction. Employees need to be motivated to do more than what is expected of them. It is this extra effort in service that exceeds the expectations of customers. This effort can only come from employees who care about their customers and are willing to satisfy them. These actions are usually not defined in job descriptions or service standards. By recognizing the achievements of your employees, you show how much you appreciate their work and efforts. This also increases their dedication further. The best way to sustain positive behavior is by recognizing and reinforcing it.

  For example, John, an employee in your company, volunteers to work on a project in addition to his normal work responsibilities. His manager can recognize and reinforce his behavior by calling attention to it during a staff meeting. The manager should communicate to everyone the importance and appreciation of employees volunteering for projects. This acknowledgment will not only encourage John to volunteer for more projects, but also encourage his co-workers to volunteer. If you want your customers to consistently receive exceptional service, you should motivate your employees by recognizing and reinforcing their positive behavior.

Making your service memorable

The second step in creating loyal customers is making your service memorable. This happens when you differentiate your products and services from your competitors'. For this, you need to understand how the expectations of customers influence their perceptions of service.

To analyze the quality of service that your organization provides, compare the level of service expected by customers to the level actually received. When a gap exists between what they expect and what they receive, as shown in Exhibit 1-1, customers view the service as poor. When they receive what they expect, customers judge the service as good.

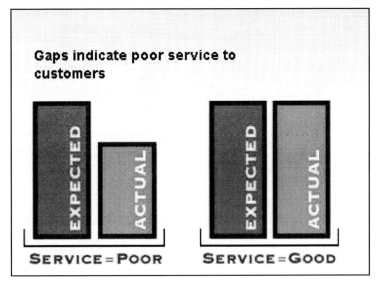

Exhibit 1-1: A graph indicating poor and good service

Building relationships with your customers

The third step in creating customer loyalty is building relationships with customers. It is important to recognize that your commitment to the customer must be the basis of this relationship. Your commitment to customer relationships will also help you to develop techniques to improve your level of service. If you do not recognize commitment as a foundation, most initiatives will end up becoming practices that are talked about, but not carried out.

When managers take action to improve service, their focus is on how their employees interact with customers. Although the service that the front-line employees provide is important, managers should also examine their ability to provide what customers need.

For example, a software company receives several complaints from customers because the customer service representatives do not spend enough time on the phone to solve their problems. The phone calls are brief because the customer service managers have implemented a policy that limits each customer phone call to 10 minutes. Although this policy was intended to decrease the cost per support call, it actually decreases overall customer satisfaction. The managers should re-examine the policy and make adjustments to make sure that customers receive the attention they need.

The leaders of service teams must demonstrate their dedication to the customer. By treating employees as customers, the leaders should set an example for employees to follow. Several actions can build relationships with your customers:

- Empower employees to provide the best service possible.
- Make follow-up calls after service transactions.
- Survey customers to determine if they are happy with the service they received.
- Ask for customer opinions on possible improvements.

Customer loyalty is an ongoing process. After creating it, you must continually monitor the ability of the company to build relationships with customers. To measure your progress, monitor the following items:

- The percentage of customers that stop doing business with you
- The amount of money spent by loyal customers over a specific number of years
- The ratio of customers who return to do business to those who do not return
- The benefits loyal customers have received from your organization through quality, time, and money

Do it!   A-2:   Creating loyal customers

Exercises

1 Sequence the steps for creating loyal customers.

   Communicate with employees

   Make your service memorable

   Motivate customers

   Build relationships with your customers

   Create dedicated employees

2 Watch the movie and then discuss the following questions:

   Discuss the importance of employee training in increasing job satisfaction.

   Discuss ways to develop dedicated employees.

3 Watch the movie. Discuss the approach of the customer service representative in creating a memorable experience for the customer.

4 Watch the movie and then discuss the following:

   Discuss how the manager's follow-up call helped to build a relationship with the customer.

   Discuss other ways to build relationships with customers.

Topic B: Market intelligence enterprise

Explanation

Marketing is the process of identifying what your customers want and developing methods to satisfy their needs. The marketing strategy of your organization can significantly contribute to its financial success. As a result, you should use a customized marketing process to establish relationships with your customers. These relationships are important because they facilitate honest feedback. This feedback measures how successful your organization is at meeting the needs of your customers.

A *market intelligence enterprise (MIE)* is a company that focuses on reaching the most profitable customers to obtain a competitive gain over other companies. The direction of an MIE is the direction that such customers decide to take, and the main goal of an MIE is to know what customers want before they do. The result is a synergy in which the company profits and the customers are satisfied.

Marketing tiers

You can use the four tiers of marketing to facilitate the development of customer relationships. These include:

- Mass marketing
- Target marketing
- Customer marketing
- One-to-one marketing

The tier structure enables the company to further narrow its customer focus.

Mass marketing

Mass marketing is the general and largest-reaching marketing tier. It entails executing major campaigns designed to reach a large number of customers and prospective customers. The company uses television, radio, magazine, newspaper, mail advertisements, and telephone solicitations to achieve mass marketing.

Although mass marketing campaigns reach a multitude of people, the response from customers is low compared to the responses generated by other forms of marketing. This is because the audience is untargeted. Mass marketing focuses on the number of relationships developed and the number of purchases generated, not on the quality of relationships or the profit potential that the company gets from each customer.

Target marketing

Target marketing uses a form of focused mass marketing to advertise products and services. Its goal is to market products and services to a smaller customer base by focusing on customers who are most likely to respond positively to the marketing efforts. This customer base is determined by looking at past data, such as purchase histories.

For example, let's say you sell cellular telephones. After learning that a new feature will soon be offered to customers, you are asked to develop a marketing campaign to sell it to your existing customers. You must generate a 10 percent response rate for your company to profit from the campaign. If you fail to reach this target, the cost of making customer contacts will exceed the benefits of the campaign.

Narrow the scope of your target market to ensure a profitable campaign. Use solicitation histories to eliminate customers who have not purchased new features in past campaigns. You can narrow the market even further by contacting only those customers who responded positively to other new-feature offers, such as call forwarding and caller ID.

Customer marketing

Customer marketing focuses on creating lifetime value. It achieves this through constant improvements in the quality of products and services and multiple interactions with customers. Customer marketing focuses on marketing products and services to typical customers. Typical customers share similar purchasing characteristics. By identifying these characteristics, companies can effectively convey their marketing messages.

One-to-one marketing

One-to-one marketing or personal selling between a salesperson and a customer is the most focused marketing tier. It is one of the most successful forms of promotion. Personal selling enables an organization to target the best customer. The interactive nature of one-to-one marketing provides immediate feedback that sales personnel can use to tailor their messages to meet specific customer needs.

The impact of personal selling is apparent throughout an organization. For example, the sales figures of a company are typically linked to the success of the sales personnel. As more products or services are sold, the company's revenue increases. The product development and marketing teams of an organization can also benefit from personal selling.

Because salespeople are in direct contact with consumers, they are familiar with the needs of customers. By analyzing customer information, the organization can effectively develop and market products and features that meet consumer demands.

An interactive communication and friendly rapport between sales personnel and customers can generate long-term relationships, increased sales orders, and opportunities for future sales. These direct contacts also enable an organization to modify their products and services, meet consumer demands, and adjust marketing efforts to reach their target markets.

Do it!   B-1:   Identifying marketing tiers

Exercises

1 Identify the four tiers of marketing by their descriptions: mass marketing, target marketing, customer marketing, and one-to-one marketing.

Creates lifetime value by continual quality improvements in products, services, and multiple customer interactions

Targets the best customer candidates and provides immediate feedback that facilitates tailored messages

Entails executing major campaigns reaching a large number of customers and prospects

Markets products and services by focusing on customers who are most likely to respond positively

2 Select the focus areas of mass marketing campaigns.

A Quantity of purchases per customer

B Customer profit potential

C Number of purchases generated

D Number of developed relationships

E Quality of products or service sold

F Quality of developed relationships

3 Select the focus of customer marketing campaigns.

A Creating a personal relationship with each customer

B Creating a lifetime value with customers

C Increasing the profit potential of the organization

D Increasing the total number of customers

4 Identify why one-to-one marketing is one of the most successful forms of promotion.

A It enables companies to develop universal marketing strategies.

B It enables companies to develop better communication avenues.

C It enables companies to target customers that don't provide profits.

D It enables companies to target the best customer candidates.

Goals of an MIE

Explanation   To foster a one-to-one marketing relationship with customers, your organization must establish specific marketing and strategic goals. Developing your company into a market intelligence enterprise will facilitate the achievement of your customer-focused goals and strategies.

The MIE that strives to achieve profitability and overall customer satisfaction must carefully outline the direction to be taken and the resources needed depending on the demands of customers. An MIE should strive to meet four main goals:

- Use customer information
- Focus on each transaction
- Use information throughout the enterprise
- Manage customer communication channels

Using customer information

An MIE uses customer information to foster customer satisfaction, which results in higher profits. Traditionally, companies used only the information provided by customers during the negotiation stages to persuade the customer to make the purchase. Companies cannot rely on partial information to gain a competitive advantage in the present marketplace.

Information sources determine the marketing direction the firm should take with specific customers. An MIE uses information acquired from each customer contact. The ultimate goal is to convert high-profit, short-term customers into lifelong partners.

Market intelligence enterprises incorporate past customer experiences with data gathered from outside the organization. The customer experiences include surveys, solicitation calls, and past purchases. External sources include credit agencies, demographic statistics, marketing companies, and motor vehicle registries.

Focusing on each transaction

An MIE views each transaction with customers as an opportunity for success or failure. Because it takes only one mistake or dissatisfying moment to influence a customer to seek the products of a competitor, each customer interaction needs to be viewed as a pivotal experience in the life of the customer with the organization.

Each transaction provides an opportunity for the company to gather more information about the customer, sell products or services, and develop the relationship of the company with the customer. For example, if a customer calls the company to ask how a product should be used, then the company knows the following information about that customer:

- Is comfortable using the telephone to contact the company
- Has difficulty understanding how to use the product
- Is willing to seek advice from a customer service representative

Seeing the response of the customer to the representative's instructions, the company realizes that the customer learns better by listening to directions, rather than by reading them in a user manual. The company also knows the attitude of the customer towards seeking advice. The phone call also provides the company with an opportunity to cross-sell or up-sell other products and upgrades to the customer.

Using information throughout the enterprise

An MIE shifts from marketing and sales to customer service and quality assurance by using customer information throughout the organization. In the past, it was virtually impossible to manage customer data so that all members of an organization could contribute and use the data to facilitate lifelong relationships.

Database management systems enable you to store and access all relevant customer information. Marketing intelligence enterprises are achieving higher levels of success and profits by implementing strategies that use technology and knowledge to sell products, modify pricing structures, and change customer-service methods.

Managing customer communication channels

An MIE aims at managing customer communication channels efficiently. In recent times, companies and customers have been introduced to a variety of communication options: telephone, e-mail, Internet, fax, and mail. When these are coupled with the vast customer base of a corporation, managing contacts can become rather difficult.

An MIE strives to achieve an optimum level of communication with customers by implementing database management software programs. These programs integrate the various forms of communication and manage information. This helps companies remain focused on their primary goal, customer satisfaction.

Do it!   B-2:   Discussing the goals of an MIE

Questions and answers

1 Write the goals of an MIE.

2 Identify the sources used by an MIE to gather information.

   A   Motor vehicle registries

   B   Past employment records

   C   Surveys

   D   Competitor's records

   E   Solicitation call records

   F   Demographic records

   G   Credit reports

   H   Past purchase records

   I   Marketing companies

3 Identify the opportunities presented to a company with each customer interaction.

   A   Create customer loyalty

   B   Offer product rebates

   C   Gather customer information

   D   Improve customer relationships

   E   Sell products or services

   F   Enforce return policies

Unit summary: Customer loyalty

Topic A

In this unit, you learned about the **benefits** of creating **loyal customers**. You learned that loyal customers are profitable contributors to a company. You also learned that to create loyal customers, you must develop **dedicated employees**, make the services **memorable**, and build **smooth relationships** with customers.

Topic B

Next, you learned about the **marketing tiers** that facilitate the development of customer relationships. You learned about **mass marketing**, which is the largest-reaching marketing tier and also about **target marketing**, which aims to market products and services to a smaller group of customers. Then, you learned about **customer marketing**, which focuses on creating typical customers and also about **one-to-one marketing**, which is the personal selling between a salesperson and a customer. Finally, you learned about the goals of an **MIE**. You learned that an MIE is a company that focuses on reaching the most profitable customers to obtain a competitive gain over other companies.

Review questions

You are the Marketing Director of Lillian Alley Enterprises, an Icon-owned venture. Lillian Alley, the founder of the company, is a home, garden, and entertaining expert with media and retail divisions. As the head of marketing, you meet with Lillian and Greg Baldwin, her Executive Business Assistant, on a regular basis to discuss their marketing strategy.

You have recently become aware that a competing media conglomerate is grooming a well-known journalist and statesman's wife, Tat Shears, to launch a television show, syndicated column, and product line that would directly rival Lillian Alley. At this meeting, you want to recommend that Lillian Alley Enterprises develop itself as a market intelligence enterprise and discuss with Lillian and Greg which marketing tier would best serve the needs of the company.

1 Why is customer loyalty essential for the success of a company?

2 What do you think your company must do to earn customer loyalty?

3 How can you develop dedicated employees?

4 How can you make your service memorable to the customers?

5 How can customer loyalty be made an ongoing relationship?

6 What are the new marketing measures that can be undertaken to retain customer loyalty?

7 What are the benefits of mass marketing as compared to other types of marketing?

8 What are the benefits that a company can enjoy from becoming a market intelligence enterprise?

Unit 2
CRM basics

Unit time: 70 minutes

Complete this unit, and you'll know how to:

A Identify the types of customer relationship management and their goals.

B Develop a customer relationship management program.

Topic A: Customer information

Explanation

Customer satisfaction is essential for a company to succeed. Your business would fail without your internal customers, such as employees, and external customers, such as consumers and distributors. Companies use *customer relationship management (CRM)* to manage customer information and facilitate customer acquisition and devotion.

CRM makes an organization customer centric. As a result, everyone in the organization focuses on the customer. Information gathered during past encounters helps you to determine what your customers want. You can use this information to market your products and services in a way that convinces customers to purchase now and to remain long-term customers as well. The type of CRM your company uses will depend on the company's goals and objectives.

Types of CRM

CRM focuses on retention and customer development. It aims at retaining customers over a long period of time by satisfying their needs with products and services. CRM spans the entire customer life cycle, which starts with the introduction of the customer to a company and ends when either the customer or the company ceases relations.

To succeed, CRM must be a company-wide effort. Although every person within the organization, including suppliers, is responsible for implementing and maintaining CRM, it is the marketing department that will work most closely with the CRM process. Individuals in this department determine which customer information is used and how it is compiled. They are also responsible for directing the implementation of the CRM process.

Your company's goals and objectives drive your processes. There are four main types of CRM to suit the goals and objectives of various organizations:

- Acquisition
- Loyalty
- Wallet-share increase
- Retention or win back

Each CRM program focuses on a different aspect of customer relationship management and the customer life cycle.

Acquisition

Customer acquisition or prospecting is used to recruit new customers. This type of CRM segments prospective customers into groups based on shared characteristics. Segmenting helps companies focus their marketing efforts on people who are most likely to buy their products or services. It makes sure company resources are effectively used and results in a greater response to the marketing campaign.

For example, suppose ABC Company manufactures Gleen and Sheen toothpaste. To market this toothpaste to consumers in an enticing way, the company segments its market by age. The company highlights the flavor and bright colors of the toothpaste to the younger market, and the ability of the toothpaste to fight cavities, gingivitis, and bad breath to the older market. By segmenting its markets, ABC Company is likely to receive a higher response as compared to targeting a single campaign for all age groups.

Loyalty

The aim of loyalty-focused CRM is to obtain and keep loyal customers. In this type of CRM, a company determines what customers want to remain loyal. Acquiring this specific information enables companies to achieve the same level of customer loyalty as other marketing efforts, but at a lower cost. Because the efforts are more focused, the response is higher and the costs are lower.

A loyalty-focused CRM company might perform three types of analysis on customers who have left the organization and on those who might leave soon. These analyses include:

- **Lifetime value-based analysis.** Conducted to determine customers that a company deems profitable. A loyalty-focused CRM company segments these customers based on the profit that each one brings. The company might choose not to invest additional time or money into customers who are not profitable or only marginally profitable.

- **Needs-based analysis.** Conducted after the company decides which customers to pursue. This analysis enables a company to develop a customized loyalty program to retain profitable customers. These programs might offer customized billing schedules or give points as rewards for purchases exceeding a specified amount.

- **Prediction analysis.** Conducted to gather historical and demographic information that helps companies to determine which customers are likely to leave and when. This information is used proactively to retain these customers.

Wallet-share increase

Companies can use this form of CRM to increase the amount of money each customer is willing to spend. There are two types of wallet-share increase programs:

- **Cross-selling.** Entails selling of complementary products and services. For example, a telecommunications company might implement a cross-selling program, such as a free temporary subscription to cable television to its loyal long-distance customers. This free subscription might entice already loyal customers to subscribe permanently to the cable service of the firm.

- **Up-selling.** Entice customers to upgrade their current product or service. These programs are designed to identify customers who have the financial potential to increase their spending with the company. Up-selling typically uses life-stage segments, which are the segments of a customer's life cycle, to increase the number of products and services sold to a customer. For example, suppose a life insurance company wants to target customers who are most likely to increase their life insurance coverage. Many life events trigger the need for more life insurance. By implementing a wallet-share increase program, the company can target customers who are just starting a family.

Many service representatives do not realize the untouched profit potential their customers have to offer. By cross-selling or up-selling, companies can greatly increase their profit potential. With CRM, companies can measure this potential and segment customers appropriately to increase the odds of succeeding with them.

Retention or win back

Retention or win back CRM concentrates on customer retention and winning back customers who have left the organization. By identifying the customers most likely to leave and the ones most likely to stay, a company can focus its retention efforts on profitable customers who are likely to leave. A win-back or save approach focuses on regaining those customers who have already left the organization.

Sometimes, it is not cost-effective to retain certain customers. It might even cost more time and money than the company can gain from them. Retention or win-back CRM enables an organization to separate the customers who were at one time loyal and profitable from the customers who were not loyal and profitable.

Do it!

A-1:   Discussing CRM types

Exercises

1   Identify the types of customer relationship management by their descriptions: acquisition, loyalty, wallet-share increase, and retention or win back.

Focuses on cross-selling and up-selling

Focuses on recruiting new customers

Focuses on keeping profitable customers

Focuses on developing customer devotion

2   Choose the division that is most affected by the implementation of a customer relationship management program.

A   Marketing

B   Finance

C   Research and development

D   Information technology

3   Identify the type of analysis by its description: lifetime value-based analysis, needs-based analysis, and prediction analysis.

Allows a company to use historical and demographic information to make predictions about customers

Permits a company to develop a customized loyalty program to retain profitable customers

Determines what customers a company deems profitable

CRM goals

An organization can accomplish five main goals by using CRM:

- Customer identification
- Data management
- Success measurement
- Analysis speed
- Return on investment

These goals can help your organization succeed by becoming more customer focused.

Customer identification

CRM improves your ability to identify profitable customers. According to the *Pareto principle*, 80 percent of the profit that a company makes is derived from only 20 percent of its customers. CRM isolates these profitable customers so that the company can focus the majority of its marketing and selling efforts on them. This reduces the marketing costs of the company.

To determine whether you have achieved the goal of identifying profitable customers, compare the average cost per customer solicitation prior to and after implementing CRM. The highest categories of solicitation costs are the wages of your sales force and marketing material, such as direct mailings and other advertisement material. If the cost per customer solicitation reduces after implementing CRM, you have identified your customers correctly.

Data management

CRM facilitates efficient data management. CRM software can be used to guarantee compatibility among different types of software being used in various departments within the company.

For example, Susan works for a financial institution that uses CRM to manage information. When she reviews data for Robert Johnson, a customer, she finds that he has consistently chosen to invest in mutual funds. Having identified this trend, Susan flags Mr. Johnson's account. This flag will alert Susan to contact Mr. Johnson when the expected rate of return on any mutual fund is higher than his current investments. Susan can also identify other investment opportunities based on Mr. Johnson's account, such as money market funds, individual retirement accounts (IRAs), and trust funds.

Mr. Johnson's customer information might be stored in software that is used only by the marketing department. The financial data might be downloaded from the Internet into a database that was formerly used only by the finance department. CRM software can integrate the data used by these two departments to produce ready-to-analyze reports. This allows the company to respond quickly to the changes in market conditions.

To achieve the goal of data management, you must first identify the kind of data that you currently gather. Next, you need to determine whether your current data is sufficient to effectively build and manage customer relationships. If not, you need to identify the data that you don't use, as well as the additional data that your company needs, such as customer histories, industry trends, and competitor strategies. Finally, after you have implemented CRM, you need to make sure the data and its organization is effectively managed.

Success measurement

CRM provides an accurate method of measuring success. Companies that gain new customers are unable to determine who or what convinced the customers to do business with them. CRM enables companies to obtain this type of information through mail-in surveys, courtesy calls, and Web site polls. This information can be used to reorganize marketing campaigns and serve the new customers better. CRM also helps to identify the best method for winning over the customers of competitors.

To measure success:

1 **Establish a benchmark.** Analyzing your current, non-CRM measurement procedures will help you set a benchmark to analyze your new CRM processes. As a result, you'll be able to compare your performance with and without CRM.

2 **Determine to what extent your company currently measures success.** Do you track the number of customer responses to direct mail, courtesy calls, polls, and other marketing campaign strategies? Are you able to evaluate the success of each campaign?

3 **Evaluate whether your company is able to better manage campaign success.** After implementing CRM, if the level of success management is the same or lower than before, you need to re-evaluate your data storage structure and capabilities.

Analysis speed

CRM increases the speed at which information can be processed, analyzed, and reviewed. This allows companies to react quickly to the changes in market conditions and risks in investments.

For example, The Federal Reserve decreases interest rates as a result of which the mortgage rates decrease. A brokerage firm might find it profitable to advise certain customers to divest from securities offering lower rates and reinvest the money into a new house at a low interest rate. The brokerage firm can tailor financial product offerings in real time to the needs of its customers.

Before incorporating CRM into your strategies, you should calculate the average length of time it takes for your employees to analyze the data needed to efficiently manage customer relationships. Repeat this exercise after incorporating CRM. If the length of time is higher or if the organization of data is not as efficient after incorporating CRM, you need to re-evaluate the types of data and processes used to increase analysis speed.

Return on investment

CRM produces a high return on investment (ROI). *ROI ratio* is the amount of money your company saves by investing as compared to the amount of money spent on the investment. Normal ROIs range from negative percentages to positive single-digit percentages. Companies that have purchased CRM programs and calculated the ROI on them have reported figures ranging from 10 to 50 times the normal return.

To achieve a high ROI, first calculate the cost of your CRM program. These costs include the time and resources taken to:

- Research different CRM programs
- Train employees to use the CRM program
- Purchase CRM software
- Integrate CRM

After calculating the total cost for your CRM program, determine the benefits it provides and assign a monetary value to each benefit. CRM benefits can include both cost reductions and increased sales and revenues. You can examine benefits, such as:

- Reduced customer contact costs
- Increased response to marketing campaigns
- Selling products and services to loyal customers at higher prices
- Increased customer referrals
- Increased cross-selling and up-selling efforts

Your ROI will be directly proportional to the duration of the CRM. Therefore, you should perform an ROI analysis at regular intervals. For example, you can perform an ROI analysis once per quarter during the first year of implementation, then once a year after the first year. To calculate ROI, divide the total benefit derived from CRM by the total cost of implementing it.

For example, the total cost of implementing CRM is $300,000, and the total monetary value gained after one year of implementation is $325,000. This value is a combination of $200,000 in cost reductions from sales and marketing costs and a $125,000 increase in sales revenues. To calculate the ROI, you need to plug the numbers into the ROI equation:

```
CRM ROI = ($325,000/$300,000) = 1.083
```

The ROI for this CRM program is 8.3%. This means that for every one dollar invested into CRM, the company receives approximately $1.08 in benefits. As the majority of CRM costs occur during the first few months of implementation, the ROI during this time might be a negative percentage. When your initial costs decrease and your benefits increase, your ROI will improve, and the goal of high ROI will be achieved.

Do it!   ## A-2:   Identifying CRM goals

Exercises

1 Select the main goals of a CRM system.

   A   High ROI

   B   Customer identification

   C   Better strategy management

   D   Better management of information

   E   Decreased employee turnover

   F   Increased development speed

   G   Success measurement

2 Icon International is a multinational company that markets electronic goods. In a recent analysis, it has been found that the marketing costs of the company are high and that its ROI indicates a negative value. The analysis also showed that the company has gained new customers for some of its products. However, the company is unable to determine who or what convinced the customers to purchase their products.

   As a proponent of CRM, discuss how implementing it will help the company solve the issues effectively.

3 What is the first step towards achieving the goal of data management?

   A   Determine whether data is sufficient.

   B   Determine whether data is managed efficiently.

   C   Establish what data you currently gather.

   D   Determine what data you do not use.

4 Identify the elements you should monitor to make sure that you have achieved the CRM goal of increased analysis speed.

   A   The efficiency of data organization

   B   The effectiveness of employee training

   C   The quantity of new information added

   D   The average length of time taken to analyze the data

   E   The average cost per data retrieval

5 Select the meaning of an ROI result of 1.095.

   A   The company receives $1.95 as benefit for every dollar invested in CRM.

   B   The company loses 9.5 cents for every dollar invested in CRM.

   C   The return on investment for this CRM program is 9.5%.

   D   The return on investment for this CRM program is 109.5.

Topic B: A CRM program

Explanation

In the past, many companies did not consider managing customer information to be an organizational priority. However, it is becoming increasingly evident that the efficient and effective management of customer information separates successful companies from unsuccessful ones.

To guarantee success in business, you must be able to centralize various types of customer information and study the relationships among each specific piece of data. This forms the knowledge base from which companies can implement marketing strategies driven by the needs of customers. You must implement CRM into the strategies of your organization to achieve this level of customer focus.

Although the decision to become a CRM organization might be easy, implementation is not. To develop a successful CRM program, you must first recognize CRM as a continual process of managing information. CRM is not designed to be a one-time, purchase-and-implement project. It is an ongoing process, which must be implemented and maintained over time. Moreover, when your company begins the process of implementing a change, you must have the evaluation criteria in place to make sure that the change is valid. You should be able to identify warnings that might be evident during the evaluation process of CRM.

CRM process

CRM is an organization-wide strategy that affects every department. As a result, it is important to consider and evaluate each step in the CRM process. These four steps in the CRM process serve as a continuous learning cycle for customer relations:

1   Gather information.
2   Develop marketing strategies.
3   Manage customer contacts.
4   Evaluate customer responses.

These steps work together to make certain that your company receives feedback about how well its actions address the needs of your customers.

Gather information

The first step in the CRM process is gathering and analyzing customer information. Your company should choose a CRM system that enables employees to obtain relevant information in a timely manner. The CRM program must also allow you to analyze customer information, such as identifying the right customer group, segmenting those customers, and predicting their behaviors and responses.

A thorough CRM system will integrate information from a variety of sources, both internal and external. Internal sources include customer service call records, mail responses, e-mail responses, Web site visits, third-party referrals, solicitation calls, and solicitation visits. External sources include industry reports, credit information, and government records.

Develop marketing strategies

The next step in the CRM process is to develop customized marketing strategies. The CRM process transforms the information gathered in the first step into logical, readable, and usable formats. The marketing department can analyze these formats to develop customized marketing strategies, such as information-delivery channels, special offers, and solicitation-contact schedules.

Manage customer contacts

The third step in the CRM process draws on the information gathered in step one and the marketing strategies developed in step two. Before you can contact customers, you need to identify the customers that you wish to target and contact.

You should also determine when to contact customers. This will depend on where they are in the customer life cycle or purchase decision process. You also need to decide which communication vehicles to use when initiating contact and what to say after you make contact.

Evaluate customer responses

The final step in this process is evaluating the responses of customers to your actions. To evaluate responses, you need to obtain feedback from your customers about their interactions with your company. Feedback can be of two types:

- **Explicit feedback.** Obtained from direct contact with customers, feedback forms, and the percentage of product returns
- **Implicit feedback.** Obtained from monitoring customer behavior, such as call histories, trade downs, and attrition rates

Your company should use this feedback to modify your marketing strategies and objectives, which include processes and selling practices.

Do it!   B-1:   Discussing the CRM process

Exercises

1 Sequence the steps of the CRM process.

   Develop marketing strategies

   Evaluate customer responses

   Manage customer contacts

   Gather information

2 CRM programs enable businesses to centralize and study customer information. What does this information provide for companies?

   A   A knowledge base that they can use to study customer-employee relationships to determine their progress

   B   A knowledge base that they can use to analyze customer information, enabling them to evaluate their core competencies

   C   A knowledge base from which they can implement marketing strategies driven by the needs of customers

   D   A knowledge base of customer data that they use to implement company-wide strategies to fulfill goals and objectives

3 What should you do to evaluate customer response for your actions?

Impact of a CRM system

Explanation   Incorporating CRM into the strategies of your organization offers many benefits. For example, by integrating large, dynamic databases into existing technologies, CRM can help your company manage its customer contacts more cost efficiently than traditional methods. These databases provide ways to gather, organize, and filter information at a faster rate as compared to departmental information databases.

Your company can also benefit from CRM in the form of time and money saved. CRM saves time because it provides easier access to customer information as compared to traditional customer management technologies. It saves money by segmenting customers into different target markets.

By using CRM to segment loyal customers from casual customers, your company can achieve a sustainable competitive advantage. The cost of acquiring a new customer is generally six times more expensive than maintaining an existing customer. As a result, retention and development efforts focused on existing customers tend to be more profitable than customer acquisition and reacquisition programs.

Companies that do not use CRM are unable to segment their customers thoroughly. They waste a considerable amount of time and money in unfocused marketing efforts. Consequently, companies that use CRM generally achieve a sustainable, competitive advantage.

Your organization might experience five main advantages by using a CRM system:

- Increased ability to thrive in a global business environment
- Increased ability to handle deregulation because of global market
- Increased competitive advantage
- Increased profit margin per customer
- Decreased customer retention and acquisition costs

Challenges of implementing CRM system

Although CRM systems have many advantages and opportunities, the company might experience several challenges if the system is not implemented properly. These challenges can cause the system to fail:

- Refusal to view CRM as a company-wide approach
- Lack of executive support
- The information technology department's lack of knowledge about the CRM system
- Poor network infrastructure
- Viewing CRM only as a system that facilitates increased automation

Do it!   B-2:   Recognizing the impact of a CRM system

Questions and answers

1   Select the benefits that CRM programs offer.

   A   Increased customer empowerment

   B   Lower employee turnover

   C   Higher inventory turnover

   D   Time saved

   E   Money saved

2   What are the main advantages of using CRM systems?

   A   Increased customer purchases

   B   Increased profit margin per customer

   C   Decreased employee turnover

   D   Increased competitive advantage

   E   Increased ability to handle deregulation as a result of the global market

   F   Decreased customer retention and acquisition costs

   G   Increased ability to thrive in a global business environment

3   List the challenges of CRM implementation.

Types of critical success factors

Explanation

Critical success factors (CSFs) are the evaluation criteria developed before any change is implemented. Developing CSF makes certain that your company evaluates the various aspects of the change, including its effects on different departments and processes. If the change does not meet the evaluation criteria, it might need to be revamped depending on the importance of the criteria and the reason for its failure. You should involve every department in the evaluation process.

Before incorporating CRM into your company, it is important that you develop CSFs to make sure a thorough evaluation of the program takes place. If a specific CRM program does not meet your criteria, you might need to consider using a different program. You might need to wait for new technologies before you can implement a CRM system that completely fits the needs of your organization.

To choose the right CRM system, you need to evaluate the following five types of CSF:

- Strategic
- Internal
- Provider
- Information technology
- User

Strategic CSFs

Strategic CSFs pertain to the organization's overall goals for the CRM system. Ask these questions to make sure that a CRM system achieves your strategic CSFs:

- What is the overall vision of your company for CRM?
- What strategic goals should the CRM system achieve?
- What contact methods should the CRM system support?
- Will the CRM system improve the overall effectiveness of the company?
- Will the CRM system facilitate communication between internal and external customers?
- Will the CRM system protect the confidential information of the company?
- Does the company have the technical resources or the finances to purchase the technical resources needed to support the CRM system?
- Do the employees have the time, dedication, and motivation to guarantee a successful CRM system?

Internal CSFs

Internal CSFs pertain to the internal operations of your business. These questions will guide you toward a system that can handle the internal CRM requirements of your company:

- Will the CRM system be able to answer most business questions within 24 hours?
- Is the company prepared to accept the risk of the CRM system failing?
- Does the company have a backup plan if the CRM system fails?
- Will the CRM system affect the mission and vision of the company?

Provider CSFs

You should also consider the CSFs of the CRM software provider when choosing a CRM system. Because CRM software is expensive, first contact and interview the references that the vendor has specified, especially the customers of the vendor, before contracting with that CRM vendor. You might ask the following questions:

- How long have you worked with the vendor?
- What value has your CRM system provided?
- Have you experienced any major problems with your system?
- Was the vendor able to offer technical assistance?
- What positive results has your system provided?
- What negative results has your system provided?
- What was the ROI of the CRM system after one year?
- Would you recommend doing business with the vendor?

Information technology CSFs

IT CSFs deal specifically with the technology parameters your company needs to make the best use of the CRM system. Before choosing a CRM system, you should ask your IT staff these questions:

- How many processors will the CRM system need?
- How much information will the CRM system hold?
- What type of information will the CRM system support?
- Does the system have a backup or recovery plan in case of a disaster?
- How many people can use the system at one time?
- How is data entered?
- What data sources are supported by the CRM system?
- How is data retrieved from the system?

User CSFs

User CSFs pertain to the information that your employees need to facilitate the development of customer relationships. This is a list of questions you should ask your users:

- What are your expectations of the system?
- What is the maximum turnaround time for information you expect the CRM system to provide?
- What information do you need to retrieve from the CRM system?
- When do you need the CRM system to be fully functional?

Do it!

B-3:   Analyzing CSFs

Exercises

1 Icon International has decided to implement CRM as a part of the company strategy. To decide the CRM that best suits company requirements, the company needs to perform a CSF evaluation. This will make sure a thorough evaluation of changes that occur in the company along with their effects on different departments and processes takes place.

   The company has developed a set of questions that will help you choose the best CRM for your company.

   As a CRM proponent, you need to classify the questions under five types of CSFs.

2 What is the most important thing you must do before contacting a CRM vendor?

   A   Contact former employees of the vendor

   B   Request a credit report from the vendor

   C   Interview the vendor's references

   D   Perform a background check on the vendor

Precautions while choosing the CRM system

Explanation

Having considered the five critical success factors for your organization, you are ready to purchase and implement your CRM system. Before making your final decision, consider the following warning signs that become evident during CSF evaluations:

- Vendor references are not solid.
- Vendor does not show up to meetings on time or at all.
- Vendor does not provide a warranty on the system.
- Technology needed to support the CRM system has not been released in the market.
- Users are not interested in the CRM system.
- Backup support plans do not exist.

If any of these warning signs are present, you might need to do one or more of the following:

- Find a different vendor.
- Purchase new technology.
- Hold a company-wide conference to explain the benefits of CRM.
- Find a CRM program that offers backup support.

Do it!

B-4:   Identifying precautions

Exercises

1   If any warning signs become apparent regarding a specific CRM system, what are some of your options?

   A   Redirect your strategies.

   B   Choose a system that offers back-up support.

   C   Contact your attorney.

   D   Choose a new vendor.

   E   Hold a company-wide conference.

   F   Purchase new technology.

2   One of the warning signs to look for during CSF evaluations is the vendor not providing a warranty on the system. True or false?

Unit summary: CRM basics

Topic A

In this unit, you learned about the different types of **CRM**. You learned that **acquisition CRM** focuses on recruiting new customers for an organization, while **loyalty CRM** focuses on obtaining and keeping loyal customers. Next, you learned that companies use the **wallet-share increase CRM** to increase the amount of money each customer is willing to spend and use **retention** or **win back CRM** to concentrate on retaining and winning back customers who have left the organization. Then, you learned about the **goals** of CRM, which will help your organization become more customer focused.

Topic B

Finally, you learned about the four steps in the **CRM process**. You learned that the first step in the CRM process is to gather and analyze customer information, and then the CRM process transforms the gathered information into **logical**, **readable**, and **usable** formats. The third step in the CRM process is to manage **customer contacts**, and the final step involves evaluating the **responses** of **customers** to your actions. You also learned about the **benefits** that an organization enjoys by implementing a CRM system and the **challenges** that might result in the failure of the system.

Review questions

1 Identify the definition of customer relationship management.

A An approach companies use to manage marketing information in a way that facilitates increased sales and decreased stakeholder turnover

B An approach companies use to manage strategic information in a way that facilitates synergy between internal and external stakeholders

C An approach companies use to manage customer information in a way that facilitates customer acquisition and devotion as well as company revenues

D An approach companies use to manage customer information in a way that facilitates increased revenues and decreased expenses

2 One of the main goals of CRM is to increase the speed of information analysis. What benefit does this specific goal provide for an organization?

A Companies can quickly react to changes in market conditions and risks in investments.

B Companies can quickly react to the strategies of their competitors and remain at the top in the industry.

C Companies can quickly react to the changes in the economy and incorporate these changes in their strategies.

You are a Sales Representative for ConTrol-Tac Systems, an Icon-owned CRM systems provider. You are invited by the Director of Marketing to meet with the officials from Battlin College. The college is interested in using your CRM software to manage information that pertains to three different customer groups: prospective students, current students, and alumni.

If the meeting is successful, they will recommend a follow-up meeting with the President of the college.

3 How does CRM benefit an academic environment?

    A CRM will help you stay competitive and manage changes in academia more efficiently.

    B The advantages of CRM will be felt throughout the company, even in areas that have nothing to do with recruitment, retention, and alumni relations.

    C As you'll spend less in student recruitment and retention, you'll yield a higher profit margin per student.

    D By reducing the amount spent to attract and keep students, you'll notice a gain in the profit margin per capita.

4 How can you evaluate the success of a CRM system?

5 What are the user CSF questions that you should ask when choosing a CRM system?

Unit 3

Preparations for CRM

Unit time: 60 minutes

Complete this unit, and you'll know how to:

A Manage and reduce costs associated with CRM implementation.

B Plan CRM implementation.

Topic A: CRM and expenditures

Explanation

CRM is an expensive investment and so due care must be taken on its economic impact on the organization. You need to know about the costs associated with CRM. You also need to know about the operational costs that can be reduced by CRM implementation.

CRM costs

Although the cost of a CRM program might vary depending on the program and the company, there are five main costs associated with CRM:

- Research
- Training
- Software
- Integration
- Maintenance

Research costs

Research costs are costs related to choosing a CRM system for your company. To be effective, your entire company must support CRM. The project manager conducts a needs-based analysis to determine the needs of each department in relation to customer information. Although this research expends time and money, it helps to guarantee the successful implementation of CRM.

You'll also need to research several CRM software vendors to find the program that works best for your company. Moreover, to gain new perspectives on the best use of CRM, you should analyze other companies in your industry that are using it. Other costs associated with research include travel costs, staff time, and presentation materials.

Training costs

Training costs are related to training employees to use the CRM system. CRM is an approach that must be understood and used by employees at every level of your organization. As a result, you'll need to conduct orientation training sessions and ongoing training sessions, which will increase costs related to staff time, presentation materials, and salaries for the trainers.

Software costs

Staff time and material resources will be used to create functional and design specifications for the user interface, server, and actual information database prior to contacting a CRM software vendor. In addition, you might need to purchase computers and related equipment to facilitate the implementation of the CRM software. After you have installed the software, you'll need to test it.

Staff time, documentation, travel arrangements, and new hardware and software purchases are some of the costs directly linked to testing CRM software.

Integration costs

Integration costs are the costs associated with converting data from the old data management system to the CRM system.

The costs of conversion can be extensive if your previous data management methods were poorly managed. In such cases, you need to transfer data from several department-specific software programs into one CRM software program and then organize it.

Maintenance costs

Maintenance costs are the costs associated with maintaining your CRM program. You need to continually update and train your employees, old and new, on the new CRM processes and goals.

Your training plan can include a CRM help desk for support services, which might include office space, staff, and other resources. Hiring CRM administrators to oversee the development and day-to-day upkeep will also increase your maintenance costs.

Do it!   A-1:   Analyzing CRM costs

Exercises

Icon International has decided to implement CRM as their company strategy. However, the board of directors is concerned about the expenditure involved in its implementation.

Which of the following are costs associated with CRM?

A   Research

B   Training

C   Software

D   Supplier

E   Integration

F   Maintenance

G   Shipping

1 Discuss the entities associated with each type of cost.

2 What type of analysis does a project manager conduct to ensure effective research?

A   Time-effectiveness analysis

B   Needs-based analysis

C   Cost/benefit analysis

D   Value-based analysis

3 Which one of the following cost categories includes creating functional and design specifications?

A   Maintenance cost

B   Training cost

C   Integration cost

D   Software cost

E   Research cost

Economic impact

Explanation

To gain the approval of the upper management and board of directors, you might need to reduce costs in other departments. This needs to be implemented before incorporating CRM into your strategies. Implementing a CRM approach helps you to reduce operational costs in five areas:

- Inventory
- Physical assets
- Distribution
- Services
- One-to-one marketing

Inventory

The cost of maintaining an inventory can be extensive for companies that sell many products. CRM helps reduce this cost of inventory.

CRM increases customer identification by determining what products customers want and when. This information can even help your company to switch to a just-in-time (JIT) inventory system. JIT inventory systems enable companies to reduce the amount of storage space they need for finished goods. Products are created only when customers need them, and they are no longer held in large quantities, regardless of current customer demands.

Physical assets

CRM can also help reduce the cost of the physical assets of your company. By reducing inventory, you can reduce the number of plants and warehouses needed to store inventory and equipment.

CRM software also facilitates electronic storage of information. After data has been entered into the CRM software, companies can discard physical copies of information, provided a sufficient backup system is in place to guarantee the security and stability of data.

Distribution

CRM can also affect product distribution. In conjunction with inventory, CRM can help reduce the rate at which products are returned along with the frequency of out-of-stock merchandise. This reduction decreases shipping costs through coordinated efforts between your company and its distributors. These reductions in cost can increase customer purchase cycle times and revenues.

CRM also affects distribution by reducing operational costs. Companies spend a great deal of money on distributors that market and sell products. CRM helps you identify distribution channels that convey your marketing message to the target market most effectively. As a result, you can save money by discontinuing distribution channels that are not profitable for your company.

Services

CRM also helps to reduce costs related to customer services. CRM is an approach that creates loyal customers. Because loyal customers need less customer service assistance than customers who are not loyal, you can focus your efforts on retaining loyal and profitable customers.

This reduction in customer service assistance reduces service costs. Moreover, timely accessibility of customer information enables sales personnel to shorten the time needed to close a sale and complete a transaction.

One-to-one marketing

CRM will improve your company's ability to manage one-to-one relationships with its customers. Implementing a one-to-one marketing approach also reduces marketing costs, as it is the most focused form of marketing. This form of marketing helps companies to develop a relationship with each customer.

Although one-to-one marketing can be costly because of the increased time and effort spent on each customer, these campaigns are generally more cost effective than mass marketing campaigns. Mass marketing does not focus on a specified target market. It uses direct mailings and massive telecommunication solicitation strategies that can consume the advertising and marketing budgets of a company.

On the other hand, one-to-one marketing campaigns focus on specific customers and their needs. They save money by not advertising to customers who are unlikely to purchase products or services from your company.

Do it!

A-2:   Discussing the economic impact of CRM

Questions and answers

1 Implementing CRM will reduce the operational costs of which of the following areas.

A   Physical assets

B   Inventory

C   Accounting

D   Customer service

E   Services

F   One-to-one marketing

D   Distribution

2 Why is one-to-one marketing more cost effective than mass marketing?

3 Which of the following benefits would your organization enjoy by reducing the cost of physical assets?

A   Reduction in the number of inventory warehouses

B   Improvement in the quality of inventory

C   Reduction in the amount of information

D   Increase in the frequency of data retrieval

E   Reduction in hard copy storage space

Topic B: Implementation planning

Explanation

As CRM uses many resources, it is important to plan its implementation. First, you need to get the approval of your upper management team and the board of directors. In addition, you'll need support from every department in the company, not only because each one will be affected by CRM, but also because various departments play an integral role in the implementation of CRM. As a result, you need to make sure that every department supports, understands, and is willing to be a part of the CRM implementation team. The members of the team should also be aware of the failure factors of CRM and the measures that can be taken to avoid failure. It is advisable to go in for a pilot test of the elements of CRM before implementation.

CRM implementation team and its functions

Your CRM implementation team is responsible for overseeing the planning and execution of CRM. This team should consist of members of your organization who will be affected by its implementation. You should recruit the following two types of team members for your CRM implementation team:

- Primary
- Secondary

Primary members

These members need to be involved in the entire implementation process. Members of this group should include employees who spend most of the time with customers, including sales and marketing representatives, as well as inbound and outbound customer service representatives. You should also include a senior IT manager who will be able to advise you about your company's information technology, as well as install and implement the CRM software. Your team might also include people from human resources, purchasing, manufacturing, and accounting departments depending on their use of CRM on a daily basis.

Secondary members

These members generally do not attend every CRM planning meeting. Instead, they are used as resources when the primary members need information. Your secondary team should consist of members working in sales, customer service, marketing, human resources, logistics, purchasing, manufacturing, and accounting departments. These members should be average workers and not just the top-performing employees because your CRM system must help everyone better manage customer relationships.

The purpose of the CRM implementation team includes:

- Strategy modifications
- Functional role changes
- Process changes
- Technology requirements
- Employees' orientation

Strategy modifications

Strategy modifications might be needed to change the direction of a company and improve its ability to manage customer relationships. Your implementation team needs to develop new strategies and objectives that will facilitate the transition from a traditional to a CRM organization.

Functional role changes

These changes will be based on your CRM strategies and objectives. For example, in the past, your customer service department was asked to limit customer phone calls to 10 minutes. This policy prevented customer service representatives from completely addressing all the needs of the customers. By implementing CRM, your new policy is to address all customers' questions before ending phone conversations. Your implementation team is responsible for developing and communicating all functional-level role changes to the appropriate employees.

Process changes

The implementation team is also responsible for communicating all process changes brought about by CRM. Each department must understand its role in these new processes. The changes will be based on the new CRM strategies and objectives, which might change the way you allocate time and resources. For example, you might need to allocate more time and resources to customer retention than to customer acquisition.

Technology requirements

As CRM needs easy access to customer information, your implementation team should examine the types of technology you'll need to accomplish this goal. Technology requirements can include a CRM software program as well as a program that will transfer data from your current system to the new system. Members of the implementation team will also be responsible for showing employees how to use the new CRM system.

Employees' orientation

Incorporation of CRM can be intimidating and stressful for the employees of the organization. The implementation team is expected to orient employees to the new company focus by holding training sessions and offering assistance to new CRM users.

Do it!   B-1:   Selecting the CRM implementation team

Exercises

1 Why are the departments in your company likely to experience functional role changes because of implementing CRM?

   A   CRM companies must make sure that every department remains on budget.

   B   CRM companies must make sure that every department is focused on mission statement.

   C   CRM companies must make sure that every department focuses on the customer.

   D   CRM companies must make sure that every department supports CRM.

2 How are secondary members used in a CRM implementation team?

3 Identify the two types of CRM members with their description: secondary members, key members, informal members, and primary members.

   These members should be typical workers because you want your CRM system help everyone not just the top-performing employees better manage customer relationships

   Members of this group include employees who spend most of the time with customers, including sales and marketing representatives, as well as inbound and outbound customer service representatives

Departments affected by CRM implementation

Explanation

Before implementing CRM, all departments within your company, including the CRM implementation team, must understand how CRM will affect their department. There are the six main departments or groups that are affected by CRM:

- Sales
- Marketing
- Customer service
- Upper management
- Information technology
- Production

Sales

The job of a sales representative in a CRM-based company is different from that in a traditional, corporate, or product-focused firm. Under CRM, sales personnel are typically focused on the customer instead of a single product or service.

The available customer information can help the sales group understand customer needs to better focus on the most appropriate products and services for each customer. This information tends to increase the win or close rate for the sales groups and reduces the amount of time needed to close a sale.

Besides selling products and services to customers, sales representatives need to gather customer information and manage individual customer relationships, not just territories. Sales representatives need to document all their transactions with the customer in the CRM software.

Sales representatives might resent CRM because they do not want to document every aspect of their jobs. You should explain to your sales team that you are not keeping this documentation solely to monitor the performance of the team, and that a detailed documentation is needed under the CRM approach to manage customer relationships better.

Another factor that will affect the sales department is the number of sales representatives needed to cover a specified area. As CRM centralizes information and enables easy retrieval methods, the number of sales representatives needed to manage your territories might decrease.

Marketing

Marketing departments too will be affected by CRM. As CRM encourages organizations to use one-to-one marketing, the focus is on each customer relationship. This will decrease traditional media advertising and increase the need for customer data management. CRM also wants the marketing department to pay more attention to the needs of the customers and be flexible in its strategies and campaigns.

Customer service

In traditional companies, the customer service department is usually under the accounting department. Because the customer service department plays a major role in developing customer relationships, companies using a CRM approach transfer the customer service department from accounting to sales or marketing.

The responsibilities of the customer service representatives also increase because they have access to customer-related information. This information empowers them to improve relationships with customers by solving their problems and promoting new products and services.

Upper management

Another group affected by CRM is upper management. Upper managers are involved in the CRM process from the beginning because they are the ones who approve its implementation. They must support CRM and help it to succeed. If they do not support CRM, middle and lower managers might feel discouraged, and this discouragement will trickle down to the front-line employees. Discouraged employees are not likely to use CRM to its full advantage, and can cause the system to fail.

The focus of the strategies, goals, and objectives of the organization will also change from being upper management-centric to customer-centric. This change in focus will affect upper managers the most because they will need to make strategic-level decisions based on the strategies, goals, and objectives of CRM.

Information technology

The IT department will work closely with the sales and marketing departments to implement technology that will help them become customer focused. Rather than using data to monitor employees and processes, IT will use it to improve customer relationships. It will structure information to satisfy customers.

The IT group facilitates the acquisition and accessibility of customer information. For this, you need to integrate different customer information from various departments such as sales, marketing, and customer service and make it accessible to all the departments. This prevents *corporate amnesia* or the loss of customer information, which occurs when a customer moves from one part of an organization to another.

Production

Traditional production departments manufacture products based on the sequence of orders in which they were received. Conversely, production departments in CRM companies base production schedules on the value of each customer. They also emphasize on-time delivery more than cost efficiency.

Do it!   B-2:   Identifying departments affected by CRM

Exercises

1 What are some new tasks that a sales representative can expect to undertake as a result of CRM implementation?

   A   Providing technical assistance

   B   Documenting transactions

   C   Developing marketing campaigns

   D   Managing customer relationships

   E   Providing legal advice

   F   Gathering customer information

2 What is the main role of the IT department in ensuring the success of CRM?

3 Match the departments affected by CRM with the changes those departments will experience: sales, marketing, customer service, upper management, information technology, and production.

   Will focus on the customer

   Will base schedule on customer

   Will rethink company focus

   Will restructure data format

   Will be equipped for service

   Will be flexible with efforts

CRM program failure

Explanation   It is important to implement CRM correctly. As only 25 percent of all CRM implementations are successful, you need to know why CRM programs fail and how to avoid failure. A CRM program might fail for any of the following reasons:

- Lack of implementation planning
- Lack of upper management support
- Unfulfilled expectations
- Focus on software instead of strategies
- Underdeveloped critical success factors

Lack of implementation planning

The first reason a CRM program might fail is the lack of implementation planning. Because customer relationship management needs many resources, you need to plan its implementation very carefully. In the absence of a plan, you might end up without the right amount of resources and staff. Planning will make sure that you do not waste time and resources.

Lack of upper management support

As CRM programs can fail due to the lack of support from the upper management, you must gain the approval of the upper management before implementing CRM. When implementation begins, you need to ask upper managers to shift from a corporation- or inward-focused strategy to a customer-focused one.

For example, one of your CRM strategies calls for a decrease in direct mailings. Your upper management team might resist this strategy because direct mailings are an inexpensive form of marketing. To combat this lack of support, you should involve upper management throughout the CRM process. Take time to explain all your CRM strategies and the effects of implementing each one. Involving upper management at this level will make certain that your CRM program does not fail because of lack of support from them.

Unfulfilled expectations

This situation occurs when your CRM program does not meet your CSFs or when the program does not achieve its goals.

To prevent unfulfilled expectations, you need to outline realistic CSFs and goals. Then, establish a process to achieve them. Finally, you should continually monitor the progress of your CRM program.

You can measure different phases of CRM implementation before it is fully implemented. These initial or interim measures provide information about the program's performance and the areas that need to be improved.

For example, rather than measuring ROI for the entire CRM program, you might determine whether the retention strategy being implemented has reduced attrition or increased the revenue or profit per customer. Alternatively, you could determine if the implementation of different portions of the CRM software has reduced the time needed to resolve a customer's problem or close a sale.

Focus on software instead of strategies

CRM programs can fail if companies focus only on the software aspect of CRM and not on strategies. Although CRM software is an important tool, CRM is a total approach for managing customer relationships. The software should be used to support CRM, not in lieu of it.

To decrease the chances of failure due to a strict focus on software, use your software to gain information about your customers and facilitate a one-to-one relationship. Closely follow your CRM strategies and use them to develop personal, one-to-one relationships with your customers.

Underdeveloped CSFs

CRM programs might also fail if CSFs are underdeveloped. CSFs are created to evaluate CRM before it is implemented. Underdeveloped CSFs might lead you to purchase a CRM system that is inadequate for the needs of your company.

For example, you did not check the references of your CRM software provider prior to purchasing the system. Six months after the purchase, you discover a fault in the system, which allows the software to assign the same customer identification number to two different people. As a result, Customer A was invoiced for both his and Customer B's purchases. Likewise, Customer B was invoiced for both her and Customer A's purchases.

To avoid CRM failure caused by underdeveloped CSFs, you should take time to research your selection criteria. Then, use these criteria to write the CSFs. If the CRM program does not meet your criteria, you might need to consider using a different program.

Do it!

B-3:   Discussing CRM program failure factors

Exercises

In the following scenario, Don, the CRM coordinator, Pam, the Senior Marketing manager, and Patricia, the Senior Sales manager, are in the conference room. Don is trying to explain how CRM will help the organization. Pam and Patricia support CRM until they discover that it will force a change in strategies and goals.

Don: So, as I was saying, CRM can really help our company manage relationships with our customers. However, it's not as easy as just calling ourselves a CRM corporation. We need to analyze some of our current strategies and determine whether any of them need to change in order to focus more on our customers than our company.

Patricia: I don't like the sound of that. We spent years fine-tuning our strategies. We can't just change them at the drop of a hat!

Pam: Patricia, I know it sounds a little over-the-top, but I've listened to the plan of the CRM Coordinator, and I really think it's going to work. *(To Don)* Why don't you explain how CRM will change our focus on customer service?

Don: Well, I know we've had some customer complaints about our current strategy for handling customer service calls. Currently, customer service representatives are supposed to try to limit service calls to ten minutes. If we can modify that strategy to allow our representatives to spend as much time as needed with each customer, we can decrease customer dissatisfaction. Although it will take longer, customers won't have to keep calling back about the same service question.

Patricia: Hmmm. We're talking about a major strategy shift here, but I can certainly see the benefits. Let's go over in detail how we can accomplish the new strategy without keeping customers on hold waiting for the next customer service representative.

1 Discuss the importance of gaining the approval of the upper management when implementing CRM.

2 Which of the following can decrease the chances of failure of a CRM program that focuses only on CRM software?

A   Following CRM strategies

B   Creating software guidelines

C   Recognizing software as secondary to CRM

D   Using software to gain customer information

E   Developing personal relationships with customers

D   Developing relationships with CRM vendors

3 Match the methods for combating CRM failure with the following reasons: lack of implementation planning, lack of upper management support, unfulfilled expectations, focus on software instead of strategies, and underdeveloped CSF.

Outline CSFs and goals and establish an evaluation process

Research selection criteria and write CSFs

Plan so that you do not waste time and resources

Explain CRM strategies and the effects of implementation

Use strategies to develop personal relationships with customers

Test CRM programs

CRM implementation needs an investment of time, personnel, and money. As this is a significant investment, you need to pilot test the elements of CRM before incorporating them throughout your organization.

A *pilot test project* is a practice run of your CRM system. It aims at testing the effectiveness of CRM within your company. Unforeseen obstacles can drain valuable resources, which can result in additional costs, the need to hire additional personnel, or an unprepared work force. To avoid this, you should test two elements of your CRM system:

- Strategies
- Software

Strategies

Before implementing CRM, you should test your strategies. To implement a pilot test project, pick one CRM strategy and test its effectiveness.

For example, one of your strategies is to increase your wallet share among customers. You find that the strategy is viable because your outbound customer service staff has increased the revenue and profit per customer by 25 percent over a one-month period. In addition, your win or close rate has increased 20 percent, the cost per sale has declined 12 percent, customer satisfaction ratings are constant, and the amount of customer defection or attrition is down.

Software

The CRM software is divided into sections. To test your software, select a product, service line, or a specific section from the CRM system, such as sales force automation, customer service and support, or marketing automation, and then deploy a marketing campaign to sell a product or service to your target market by using the information in the CRM software.

At the end of a specified trial period, analyze your results and compare them with your CRM goals. You need to compare the following factors:

- Your ability to identify and target specific customers
- Your ability to manage data better
- The speed at which information was obtained and used

These comparisons will help facilitate a company-wide, customer-focused approach.

For example, to review your sales force automation module, you should evaluate measures, such as administration time and data synchronization, at the end of your test period. *Data synchronization* is the ability to update and distribute information across computers that are not networked, such as laptops and other mobile machines. In addition, you should analyze the cost of sales, the win rate, and the time it takes to generate a lead and close a sale.

If you evaluate the customer service and support module, you should evaluate several measures. These measures include the average handling time, abandonment rate, time in queue before a service representative talks to a customer, time to complete a call, and the resolution rate, which is the percentage of calls where the issue is resolved.

Do it!

B-4:   Testing a CRM program

Exercises

1 What should you do to test your CRM software?

    A   Review backup tapes.

    B   Align software with strategies.

    C   Document processes.

    D   Select a product or service line.

    E   Deploy a marketing campaign.

2 Select and sequence the steps for testing your CRM strategies.

   Deploy marketing campaign

   Test effectiveness

   Select a strategy

   Determine viability

3 Sequence the steps for testing your CRM software.

   Deploy marketing campaign

   Analyze results

   Select a product

Unit summary: Preparations for CRM

Topic A   In this unit, you learned about the **costs** associated with CRM. You learned that the five main costs associated with CRM are the **research**, **training**, **software**, **integration**, and **maintenance**. Next, you learned about the **economic impact** of CRM implementation. You learned that CRM reduces **operational costs** in areas such as inventory, physical assets, distribution, services, and one-to-one marketing.

Topic B   Finally, you learned about the **CRM implementation team**, which oversees the planning and execution of CRM. You learned about the two types of team members, **primary** and **secondary**. You learned that primary members spend most of the time with customers while secondary members are used as resources when primary members need information. You also learned about the **departments** that are affected by CRM and the reasons for the **failure** of a CRM program. You also learned that before implementing a CRM system, it is imperative to test its two elements, **strategies** and **software**.

Review questions

You are offering a CRM solution to a company. Your goal is to explain how CRM can help the company achieve its goals and identify ways to modify expenditures to guarantee a customer-focused effort.

1   How do you think that using a CRM system will make a difference in the present scenario?

2   The marketing department uses outdated database software, which is incompatible with other departments. Do you think implementing CRM will be a failure in this case?

The Consumer Goods Division of Icon International has decided to implement CRM. They have created a CRM implementation team and have decided on the primary members of the team.

In preparation for the implementation process, you are meeting the primary members of the team to discuss the role that this team will play during the process, as well as the departments that will be affected by the program. Finally, you must effectively convey the reasons for the failure of CRM programs.

3   Who do you think should be included as secondary members?

4   In your opinion, how will implementing CRM effect the sales department?

5 How does implementing CRM alter the marketing process?

6 Why do some CRM programs fail to meet all the expectations of the company?

7 How do we test the effectiveness of CRM with a company?

Unit 4

CRM implementation

Unit time: 40 minutes

Complete this unit, and you'll know how to:

A Redesign your work processes, and identify reasons to implement CRM in stages.

B Implement CRM.

Topic A: CRM implementation preparation

Explanation

Implementing CRM without developing strong customer relationships can lead to failure. To avoid this, first examine the current strategic position of your company and customers and then determine the processes that you can improve. It is not advisable to implement CRM in a single step. To ensure the effectiveness of your CRM program, implement it in stages.

Redesigning your work processes

Before you redesign your work processes, you should first develop a strategy for CRM based on the relationship between your company and its customers. The strategy and the resulting work processes will help your company to establish strong customer relationships. The following steps will help you to develop a customer relationship strategy, and then help you to redesign your work processes around that strategy.

1 Gather information.
2 Define your customer base.
3 Study the external influences of customers.
4 Identify opportunities.
5 Develop CRM strategies.
6 Redesign work processes.
7 Evaluate strategy achievement.

Gather information

Before taking any measures to change work processes, gather information about your company's current work processes and its relationships with customers. You will need to examine all areas of your business. First, identify the processes that need to be changed. Next, identify those processes you have the resources and capabilities to change.

For example, on examining the accounting department you discover an opportunity for a process change. Modify the invoicing process by allowing your sales team to negotiate product prices with clients. To facilitate flexible pricing, allow the sales team instead of the accounting department to enter the invoices. A sales manager will approve any negotiated prices that fall outside the acceptable range.

As a result, when a sale is made, the salesperson enters the invoice information into the CRM software, which routes this information to accounting. It is possible to implement this process because the CRM software, which is capable of routing data to other parts of the software, is already in place.

Define your customer base

After gathering information about your processes, you need to define your customer base. Traditional marketing research entails finding out who your customers are and what they need. Many companies fail at traditional marketing because their company strategies are influenced more by upper management than customers needs. These company strategies have an internal focus and are not customer focused.

As these marketing strategies support the objectives of the upper management and not the customers, they can lead to a decrease in market position and profits and dissatisfied customers. To avoid this, you need to find out who your customers are and what they need. Effective market research can give your company a competitive advantage.

To determine your customer base, you need to document the customers who buy your products and services, as well as the characteristics of these customers. Next, divide your customers into groups based on common characteristics. These groups are known as *customer segments*. Characteristics worth examining include geographic location, age, income, education, occupation, social class, degree of product knowledge, product or service usage rate, store loyalty, and brand loyalty.

You also need to group corporate customers by industry, size, products and services used, purchase cycle, and purchase or procurement process. After grouping your customers, examine your research to identify what it is that your customers want that your company is not providing. You might need to conduct additional customer surveys to gather this information. Survey questions can include:

- What is our company doing well?
- What could our company do better?
- What is your overall satisfaction level with our company?
- What new products and services could we offer to convince you to remain loyal to our company?

Examine this information along with the characteristics of each customer segment. Finally, determine what your company can do to further encourage loyalty towards your products and services.

For example, during the implementation of its CRM program, Dell Computers grouped its customers based on the number of PCs sold, services used, and industry type. Dell found that by grouping customers according to specific characteristics, its customers were more satisfied and its operations ran smoothly.

Study the external influences of customers

Studying the external influences on your customers is the next step in redesigning the work processes. External influences are the factors that affect the decisions of your customers. Customer influences include your competitors, the current income of your customers, the state of the economy, government regulations, and societal and market trends.

After identifying these influences, examine the extent to which each one affects your customers, including whether each has a positive or negative impact on your strategies. Then, determine the measures that you need to take to capitalize on or counteract these influences.

Identify opportunities

The fourth step towards redesigning work processes is to identify opportunities that facilitate the building of strong customer relationships. Examine the information related to the process, customer, and external influences gathered in steps one to three. Use this information to identify opportunities that can lead to customer loyalty.

For example, in the first step, you determined that your company could change its inventory system, if needed. In the second step, you discovered that your customers want customized products, and in the third step, you determined that your competitors offer customized products. From this information, you can generate an opportunity to implement a just-in-time inventory system that would permit you to build customized products without wasting storage space, materials, and staff time in producing excessive amount of products.

Develop CRM strategies

After you have identified the opportunities that will help you build customer relationships, develop strategies to measure the implementation of your ideas. For example, if you decide to capitalize on the transition to a just-in-time inventory system, you might develop a strategy to increase customer acquisition by 25 percent.

Redesign work processes

After you have developed your strategies, you are ready to redesign your work processes. You should redesign only those processes for which you have the resources, opportunity, and need based on external influences and market research.

For example, to redesign your inventory system, you need to train your employees on the new process and alert other departments and customers to the change. If you do not communicate this change to your customers, they will not be aware that you are offering customized products.

You might also need to buy specialized equipment, hire more employees to produce the customized products, reduce inventory storage space, and temporarily increase advertising expenses to communicate this change to customers. Moreover, you should establish program evaluation measures to ensure agreement among team members regarding the effectiveness of the changes.

Evaluate strategy achievement

The final step is to evaluate your ability to achieve your strategies. These are some questions that you can ask yourself:

- Do the new work processes facilitate the achievement of the strategies?
- Are the new processes more effective than the old processes?
- Do the new processes permit our company to build stronger customer relationships?

If your evaluation indicates that your new work processes do not achieve your strategies or permit you to build stronger relationships with customers, verify whether you are better off with the new processes or not.

If not, consider reverting to your old processes or developing new ones that eliminate your current challenges. If your evaluation indicates that your new work processes do achieve your strategies and permit you to build stronger relationships with customers, find out whether you can improve your new processes.

Do it!   A-1:   Preparing for CRM implementation

Exercises

1 Sequence the steps that establish strategies to redesign your work processes.

Identify opportunities

Study the external influences of customers

Redesign work processes

Gather information

Develop CRM strategies

Define your customer base and direction

Evaluate strategy achievement

2 Watch the movie. Discuss the importance of gathering information when redesigning work processes.

3 Why do many companies fail at traditional marketing?

A   Customer needs influence company strategies more than the upper management.

B   Marketing influences company strategies more than customer needs influence company strategies.

C   Customer needs influence company strategies more than marketing influences company strategies.

D   Upper management influences company strategies more than customer needs influence company strategies.

4 When is it appropriate to consider redesigning your work processes?

A   When you have the resources, revenues, and feedback

B   When you have the resources, opportunities, and need

C   When you have the need, revenues, and resources

D   When you have the capabilities, materials, and opportunity

Implementing CRM in stages

Explanation

After you have determined how to modify your work processes, you are ready to implement CRM. Implementing CRM in stages gives you the following advantages:

- Less employee resistance
- Gradual introduction to customers
- Ability to monitor progress and success

Less employee resistances

It is better to gradually introduce CRM to employees. If you implement your program all at once, your employees might be more resistant to the change than if you implement it in stages. Moreover, employees are naturally hesitant about accepting big changes. As a result, by implementing CRM in stages, you can avoid these hesitations.

Communicate to your employees the details of each stage, including how and when CRM will be implemented, and how it will affect their jobs. This communication will ensure that your employees are aware of the benefits that each part of CRM offers. Consequently, you will gain the full support of your employees for CRM implementation.

Gradual introduction to customers

Another factor that you need to consider while implementing CRM is customers. Implementing CRM all at once might be too overwhelming for your customers who are accustomed to your routines. Dramatic, large-scale changes might encourage them to take their business elsewhere. By implementing CRM in stages, customers will be more likely to accept your changes. This becomes more important if your program needs customers to change communication avenues or provide more detailed, personal information. If customers are reluctant to provide personal information, you should explain to them exactly how you'll use this information.

Ability to monitor progress and success

A third factor that makes it important to implement CRM in stages is the ability to monitor the progress and success of the program. If you implement CRM all at once and the program fails, its repercussions will be more than if you implement it in stages.

Implementing CRM in stages also makes it easier for you to identify the parts of your program that are not working correctly. As a result, it is easier for you to make timely adjustments.

Do it!   A-2:   Identifying reasons for implementing CRM in stages

Questions and answers

1 Why is it best to gradually introduce CRM to your employees?

   A   Employees do not support change.

   B   Employees support current processes.

   C   Employees do not have time to manage change.

   D   Employees are naturally hesitant to accept change.

   E   Employees are naturally resistant to change.

2 Why is it best to gradually introduce customers to CRM?

3 A gradual introduction of CRM is preferred by both the employees and the customers. Do you think these are the only factors that necessitate the implementation of CRM in stages?

Topic B: The implementation process

Explanation

After redesigning your work processes and working towards implementing CRM in stages, you'll be ready to implement your CRM program.

Implementing CRM

The following steps should be used when your company starts implementing the CRM program:

1   Obtain senior-level sponsorship.
2   Gather stakeholder information.
3   Link opportunities to capabilities.
4   Define CRM project requirements.
5   Develop a business case.
6   Develop a rollout strategy.
7   Evaluate progress.

Obtain senior-level sponsorship

The first step you should do before implementing CRM is obtain senior-level sponsorship. Because CRM will need substantial financial resources, you'll need a proposal approved by your upper-management team and board of directors. This proposal should detail the costs and benefits of CRM, as well as the methods you'll use to implement it.

Beyond approving your proposal, upper management must also show full support towards CRM to make it a success. If upper management does not support CRM, middle and lower managers might feel discouraged. This discouragement can also trickle down to the front-line employees. Discouraged employees are not likely to use CRM to its full advantage, and the system could fail.

In addition, the focus of the strategies, goals, and objectives of the organization will shift from satisfying upper management to satisfying customers. This change in focus will affect upper managers because they will need to make strategic-level decisions based on the strategies, goals, and objectives of CRM.

Gather stakeholder information

After upper management has approved CRM, you need to gather information from your stakeholders. Your internal stakeholders include employees, managers, and executives who will use CRM to develop customer loyalty. External stakeholders include vendors, creditors, lenders, customers, competitors, and regulators. You'll need to gather information about external stakeholders to determine how processes, such as invoicing, will affect the CRM process.

After you have gathered this information, determine how the process changes will affect your stakeholders and communicate these changes to them. For example, your stakeholders might experience changes related to invoicing, inventory methods, and billing cycles.

Link opportunities to capabilities

In the third step of the CRM implementation process, you need to link your opportunities to your capabilities. This makes sure that your firm uses existing resources to leverage the most viable opportunities among prospects and customers. For example, leveraging the access to product and service history information available in your CRM system for customer service and support can increase customer satisfaction and loyalty.

To link your opportunities to capabilities, first list the opportunities for change that will facilitate building strong customer relationships. Then, identify the current CRM capabilities of your firm with respect to the opportunities that you have already identified. If you do not have the capabilities necessary to incorporate your opportunities, determine whether you can obtain these resources. If you cannot obtain them, you need to omit the opportunity from your list. Lastly, you need to link your opportunities to your capabilities. This will make sure that you are not allocating the same capabilities and resources to more than one opportunity.

Define CRM project requirements

The fourth step you should take when implementing CRM is to define your CRM project requirements. Because each CRM project needs resources, you need to prioritize all your projects to make certain that you have enough resources to complete them.

You need to meet both the primary and secondary members of your implementation team to specify which projects should take precedence over others. Examples of projects include detailing the sources of profits for your company, enhancing call center operations, and establishing a data warehouse.

Develop a business case

You develop a business case based on your findings in step four. A *business case* includes detailing the process and cost of each project, such as staff, training, technology, and outsourced resources. You also need to develop a projected duration for each project along with options to complete the project using internal or external resources.

For example, you need to develop a database that tracks your most profitable customers. You know that this database uses a software program that no one in your company is familiar with. As a result, you'll need to either outsource the project or train your staff on this software program. Your business case will detail your options, your decision, the time it will take to implement the project, and the cost of the project.

Develop a rollout strategy

Your next step is to develop a *rollout strategy*, which outlines the priority, time line, level of staff effort, and resources needed to complete each project. You also need to detail how you'll measure the success of each project.

This detailed information will not only allow you to evaluate the results of the entire project and the CRM, but will also make sure that everyone involved in each project supports it fully. If a member of the CRM implementation team does not support CRM or the way you are planning to implement it, then this person should communicate these thoughts at this stage instead of waiting until you have implemented the rollout strategy.

Evaluate progress

The final step in implementing CRM is evaluating your progress. Consider the goals of CRM and the benefits it is supposed to provide to your organization.

If you find that your CRM program fails to meet your goals or benefit your organization, find out ways to improve it. Some of the items to consider when a CRM program fails include:

- Choosing a new CRM program
- Choosing a different vendor
- Purchasing new technology
- Holding a company-wide conference to explain the benefits of CRM
- Finding a CRM program that offers backup support

Do it!

B-1:   Discussing CRM implementation steps

Exercises

1 What is the main goal of CRM for internal stakeholders?

   A   To decrease research time

   B   To develop customer loyalty

   C   To lower acquisition costs

   D   To decrease information storage

2 Watch the movie. Discuss how a CRM coordinator and IT department manager worked together to define CRM project requirements.

3 Identify why it is essential to prioritize your projects during a CRM implementation.

   A   To make sure that you have enough resources to complete them

   B   To eliminate non-essential projects

   C   To determine how projects should be completed

   D   To make sure that the projects are all necessary for the successful implementation of CRM

4 Why is it important to link your opportunities to capabilities?

5 During which step in the CRM implementation process, should you determine the level of effort needed to implement CRM?

   A   Obtain senior-level sponsorship.

   B   Link opportunities to capabilities.

   C   Define CRM project requirements.

   D   Develop a rollout strategy.

6 Identify the examples of detail that would be included in a business case.

   A   The cost, projected duration, and completion options for each project

   B   The cost options for each project, as well as the departments that will be most affected

   C   The process for completing the project and the specific individual responsible for implementation

   D   The anticipated process for completing the project as well as the best-and worst-case scenarios

7 Select the choice that currently identifies a benefit of including detailed information in your rollout strategy.

   A   It will make certain that everyone involved in the project fully supports it.

   B   It will make sure that everyone in the company fully supports CRM.

   C   It will make sure you monitor the progress of the projects.

   D   It will guarantee a successful implementation.

Unit summary: CRM implementation

Topic A   In this unit, you learned how to redesign your **work processes** to establish strong customer relationships. You also learned about the factors that make it necessary to implement CRM in **stages**. Next, you learned that implementing CRM in stages helps to gradually introduce CRM to employees and customers. This also helps to monitor the **progress** and **success** of the program.

Topic B   Finally, you learned about the various steps of **CRM implementation**.

Review questions

1 Identify the step you should take before beginning the CRM implementation process.

   A Determine which step of the implementation process should be done first.

   B Determine who would be the most effective person to lead the implementation process.

   C Determine what processes can be eliminated to make CRM cost-effective.

   D Determine what processes can be improved to facilitate strong customer relationships.

2 Select the option that is an appropriate characteristic to study when grouping business-to-consumer customers.

   A Standard industry code

   B Size

   C Geographic location

   D Purchase process

3 Select the factor that can be identified by a trend of decreased sales during economic downturn.

   A Education level

   B Decreased competition

   C Internal influences

   D External influences

4 Select the most viable opportunity when the majority of your customers are local, distance to outlets are prohibitive, and when effective and cost efficient delivery systems are possible.

   A You could implement a just-in-time inventory system.

   B You could set up an online retail shop to broaden your reach to potential customers.

   C You could start offering in-store discounts to out-of-town shoppers.

   D You could offer promotions to lure customers to visit from other parts of the country.

5 If you have decided to start an e-commerce Web site, what would be your strategy to measure the success of the Web site?

   A Maintain customer retention rates

   B Maintain a customer satisfaction rate of 95 percent

   C Increase new customer acquisition by 30 percent

   D Establish a more dynamic online presence

6 Give some examples of external stakeholders.

Unit 5
eCRM

Unit time: 90 minutes

Complete this unit, and you'll know how to:

A Identify the features and disadvantages of eCRM.

B Automate CRM through eCRM.

Topic A: eCRM fundamentals

Explanation

CRM focuses on making an organization customer centric. It uses communication methods, such as in-person, telephone, fax machine, and mail contacts to contact customers. In the business world today, electronic communication is a critical form of communication. *Electronic customer relationship management (eCRM)* is an electronic communications approach used by stakeholders to establish, develop, and manage relationships with customers. It helps your company communicate effectively with customers through the Internet. Communications through eCRM range from sales and customer service to electronic customer satisfaction surveys. These communications usually occur through the company's Web site. Although eCRM can be an effective way to manage customer relationships electronically, it has various disadvantages also.

CRM and eCRM

Although CRM and eCRM share the same goals and focus, they have some basic differences. eCRM is essentially an online version of CRM. It provides your company with an additional channel to communicate with your customers. Although eCRM needs more advanced technology than traditional CRM systems, the opportunities presented to customers during one visit to the company's Web site far outweigh the opportunities they experience through telephone, fax, mail, or in person.

Your company can succeed at managing customer relationships most effectively by incorporating a combination of eCRM and CRM strategies throughout the organization. For example, a successful eCRM application must support communication across multiple channels, including e-mail, telephone, fax, and in-person communications. It must also include customizable interfaces for various stakeholders such as your customers, employees, and suppliers.

eCRM as a competitive advantage

The percentage of people who use the Internet to communicate, browse for products, and make purchases is increasing. As customers appreciate the convenience offered by at-home shopping, companies whose Web sites do not permit customers to learn about their company and products, make purchases, and ask questions will be at a competitive disadvantage. Companies that use eCRM can manage online customer relationships and overall customer satisfaction better than companies that do not employ an eCRM system.

Companies using eCRM take less time to process orders, ship products, and respond to the needs of customers as compared to traditional companies. This reduced response time is the result of a central database that includes customer information related to sales, complaints, questions, and several other interactions. Companies with quick response times experience a competitive advantage over competitors that do not employ such tactics.

Do it!

A-1:   Discussing eCRM

Multiple-choice questions

1 Which of the following forms of communication are used by eCRM?

    A   Online customer satisfaction survey

    B   Telephone

    C   Company Web site

    D   In person

    E   Fax

2 Select the information that can be found in a customer database.

    A   Competitors

    B   Sales information

    C   Unlisted phone numbers

    D   Inquiries

    E   Complaints

3 Choose the definition of eCRM.

    A   Establishing customer relationships through in-person contact

    B   Using electronic communication to foster and manage customer relationships

    C   Using e-mail to manage customer relationships

    D   Tracking purchases through an online catalog site

eCRM features

Explanation

eCRM offers a company and its customers many benefits and options that cannot be provided by traditional business communication channels. Fast response times and customized interactions increase customer satisfaction and improve business efficiency. A successful eCRM application has the following four main features:

- Self-service knowledge base
- Automated e-mail response
- Online cross-selling, up-selling, and bulk discounts
- Customization of Web content

Self-service knowledge base

Self-service knowledge base is a variety of online information available on the Internet. This includes help menus and links to other Web sites that guide customers through specific interactions. As these knowledge bases are customer-led, they are customized according to their needs. They include access to information for product evaluation, literature fulfillment, product configuration, online purchases, order processing, service questions, product registrations, and product upgrades.

Automated e-mail response

Another feature offered by successful eCRM applications is automated e-mail responses to customer inquiries. If a customer purchases a product or service through your eCRM-enabled Web site, an automated e-mail response will be generated to confirm the order and its payment, provide contact information of the company if the customer has questions or further inquires, and provide an estimated time of delivery. As a result, order processing becomes an opportunity for establishing communications, also called *touchpoints*, with the customer.

When a customer enters your Web site to ask a question about a product or service, an eCRM-enabled application will guide the customer to an electronic customer inquiry form. The customer will fill out this form and include his e-mail address and the inquiry. The eCRM application will generate an automated e-mail response based on the content of the inquiry. This feature is especially helpful for requests such as catalog or literature fulfillment, which can be tailored to deliver the information needed by a prospect or customer. For example, information can be limited to a specific model or performance question. If the customer is not satisfied by the automated response, a true CRM organization will handle the inquiry through other communication channels, such as telephone, mail, or in person.

Online cross-selling, up-selling, and bulk discounts

Online product bundling and pricing is another feature provided by successful eCRM applications. Traditionally, salespersons offer special discounts to customers who buy products or services in bulk. They also succeed in cross-selling complementary products and services. For example, if Mr. Gomez walks into an electronics store to purchase a television, a salesperson might persuade him to also purchase a one-year, in-store warranty for the TV. The salesperson might also convince Mr. Gomez to buy a television stand, a DVD player, and a new sound system to go along with the TV.

eCRM permits companies to provide collaborative selling and service online, in real time, based on the purchases made by customers. For example, eCRM would provide a prompt about a TV stand, DVD player, or warranty during the order process. Cross-selling can also be done with partners who sell related products, such as a TV stand manufacturer and warranty provider.

Through a complex relationship database, eCRM applications can establish scenarios that permit companies to effectively market products and services electronically. For example, a medical supply company, Prescriptions Unlimited, is looking for a new basic software applications package. It has been a long-time customer of Software Solutions, a company that sells not only basic software, such as word processing and spreadsheet applications, but also customizable database applications.

Prescriptions Unlimited decides to place its order for the basic software package electronically. Software Solutions has incorporated an eCRM application into its Web site. As this application is linked to its back-office customer information database, the company can electronically retrieve information about the purchasing history of Prescriptions Unlimited.

The eCRM application recognizes that the customer has not yet purchased a customizable database application from Software Solutions. This package would permit Prescriptions Unlimited to synchronize the information from its word processing and spreadsheet applications with the database software. After this opportunity is triggered, the eCRM system automatically probes Prescriptions Unlimited about its current database system. This eCRM-enabled, customized advertising exposes Prescriptions Unlimited to the product and provides Software Solutions with valuable marketing information about its customer. The company can initiate further contact about this potential purchase through eCRM tactics or through traditional CRM forms of communication, such as a sales telephone call to the company.

Customization of Web content

eCRM applications provide a secure means by which stakeholders can access only the information that they need. They permit all stakeholders within a company to customize their Web content. For example, customers can customize their Web pages to show only the products and services in which they are interested. Companies can also determine special prices, discounts, and payment methods based on the value of each customer to the company.

Employees do not need the same information as customers. They might need to retrieve information related to financial data, customer purchase records, and upcoming company events. An eCRM application will permit them to access this information.

Suppliers too can access the inventory status of a company through an eCRM application. This permits companies and their suppliers to process and ship orders quickly.

Do it!   A-2:   Identifying eCRM features

Exercises

1 Discuss the following features of eCRM:

  Group A: Self-service knowledge base

  Group B: Automated e-mail response

  Group C: Online cross-selling, up-selling, and bulk discounts

  Group D: Customization of Web content

2 What type of information can a customer access from a self-service knowledge base?

  A   Literature fulfillment

  B   24-hour access to live help

  C   Service questions

  D   Information on other customers

  E   Product registrations

  F   Competitor information

  G   Online purchases

3 A customer purchasing a new music CD online receives a prompt about T-shirt, concert information for the artist, other CDs in the same musical genre, and a sale on Walkmans. What eCRM feature does this describe?

  A   Automated e-mail response

  B   Volume discounts

  C   Self-service knowledge base

  D   Cross-selling

eCRM disadvantages

Explanation

Although eCRM is effective in managing customer relationships electronically, it has its share of disadvantages too. You can avoid most of these by using it with other marketing tactics, such as regular CRM, one-to-one marketing, or a market intelligence approach. There are four main disadvantages of eCRM:

- Lack of person-to-person contact
- Inadequate feedback
- Limited customized pricing
- Delayed response time

Lack of person-to-person contact

Most communication is in the form of e-mail, such as a customer submitting a purchase form, a satisfaction survey, or a company sending solicitation e-mail. Actual person-to-person contact only occurs when the customer calls the company with a question or complaint about a specific product or service.

To overcome this disadvantage, your company can take measures to make sure that you have other forms of contact in place. For example, you can make your telephone numbers and store addresses accessible and visible on your Web site. You can also ask customers if they would prefer to receive a telephone call from a customer service representative or a letter in the mail. To increase customer satisfaction, make sure that you contact customers by using the channels they prefer.

Inadequate feedback

In a typical service or customer solicitation telephone call, the company representative can ask questions to get an idea of the customer's experience with the company. Obtaining feedback is difficult when you operate strictly on an eCRM system.

You can overcome this issue by periodically asking customers to fill out satisfaction surveys online. You can also contact them through other channels to receive more feedback if they are willing to provide it. Make sure your customer service representatives ask customers about their satisfaction with the company when they handle inquiries over the telephone.

Limited customized pricing

Successful eCRM applications can customize pricing by accessing information about the customer's purchasing history and rank as a customer. They analyze this information to determine a customized price for the specific customer. Nevertheless, this method is not exact and does not take into account the human aspect of a sale, such as negotiating the price for products and services with a salesperson.

You can implement a dynamic pricing approach to overcome the lack of customized pricing. This approach uses the customer's history, the product or service configuration being purchased, and the current purchase requirements to develop customized online pricing. All these pricing could be rule-driven and developed by the company based on the analysis of past purchases.

Delayed response time

eCRM, by itself, can delay response time in customer inquiries. For example, a customer needs to ask a question about a product or service, and the only way to contact the company is through e-mail. If the customer service representatives do not respond to customers' e-mails in a timely manner, customers might have to wait for days to receive a response. This delay in response time might be applicable to both customer e-mails and product shipping. A customer who buys a product online will have to wait longer to receive it as compared to purchasing it in person at a store. Typically, if a customer orders a product online and wants it the next day, he must pay high shipping costs.

You should enact a policy to treat e-mail inquiries with the same urgency as telephone calls or in-person visits. You might also consider offering free overnight shipping and handling for specific products to ensure that customers receive them as fast as they do by physically visiting a store.

Do it!

A-3:   Discussing eCRM disadvantages

Questions and answers
1 What are the disadvantages of eCRM?
2 Discuss a strategy to overcome each disadvantage of eCRM.
3 You can minimize the disadvantages of eCRM by using it with a market intelligence approach. True or false?

Topic B: eCRM and automation

Explanation   You can also use eCRM to automate the management of all information used by various departments in a company. The departments that can be automated by using eCRM include marketing, sales, customer service, and accounting.

Automate the marketing department

You can use eCRM to automate the following marketing processes:

- Managing customer and prospect information
- Customizing marketing efforts

Managing customer and prospect information

To place online orders, customers must enter your Web site and click the links to browse your products or services and place orders. The marketing department can gather important information about customers and prospects by tracking the type of products that interest specific customers.

For example, if you operate an online retail clothing store, you can track a variety of information about your customers, such as the styles they prefer, when they are likely to place orders for certain merchandise, and the prices they are willing to pay for the items. This information can determine the new styles that should be marketed to specific customers, the price range of products that should be targeted at them, and the inventory to be kept on hand.

Customizing marketing efforts

You an also automate the marketing department by customizing its marketing efforts. Advertising your Web site presents many new opportunities and challenges. For your Web site to gain recognition, you must target two types of customers, the browser and the solicited customer.

- **The browser.** This type of customer finds your Web site while searching for a specific type of product or service. The typical browser visits one or more of the top five search engines on the Internet, types in a few key words, and visits the top sites listed in the results. To reach these customers, you must continually update your *META tags* or the lists of key words you must submit to search engine sites. Carry out research to determine the key words that will direct customers to your site. As different key words can draw different customers or prospects, diversify your list. For example, if your company operates an online retail clothing store, some of your key words might include slacks, pants, denim, jeans, jackets, shirts, dresses, and shoes. The more comprehensive and organized your list of META tags, the higher your site is placed on the list of search results.
- **The solicited customer.** This type of customer visits your Web site after seeing your URL or Web site address in traditional forms of advertising, such as television ads, radio ads, mailings, and word-of-mouth referrals. To appeal to these customers, make the URL visible in your traditional advertisements, and promote the quality and ease-of-use of your Web site. You should also explore the option of e-mailing advertisements to customers and prospects. Although e-mail permits you to tailor the content of your advertisement, promotion, or offer, you must be careful because solicitation e-mails can be a nuisance for the recipients and might lose customers.

Impact on other departments

Automating your marketing processes also benefits departments in your company, such as:

- **Finance department.** Obtains valuable forecasting information from Internet customer databases.

- **Sales department.** Gains vital insight concerning what customers want and when they want it.

- **Production department.** Receives data on what products to make, including styles, colors, sizes, and quantities.

- **Accounting department.** Has less information to enter into computer systems because online customers enter their own payment information. When this information is entered, eCRM software automatically generates the appropriate accounting transactions. This reduces time spent by staff on billing and recording accounting information.

Do it!

B-1:   Automating the marketing department

Questions and answers

1 When managing customer and prospect information, what kind of items can a marketing department track?

   A Past purchases from competitors

   B Employment history

   C Price range of past products

   D Preferred styles

   E Complaints

   F Purchase cycle for certain items

2 Which of the following marketing processes can be automated by using the eCRM program?

   A Managing customer and prospect information

   B Customizing marketing efforts

   C Customizing the yearly goals of marketing

   D Managing competitor information

   E Tracking complaints

3 What strategy do you think is the best to give up-to-date product information to the customers?

4 If Petstuff is the name of your online pet supply store, which of the following are the best META tags to direct customers to your site.

   A Paint

   B Frisbees

   C Slacks

   D Videos

   E Birds

   F Flea powder

   G CDs

Automate the sales department

Explanation   Your sales department can also use eCRM to automate some of its processes, such as:

- Managing sales information
- Fulfilling literature requests
- Configuring products online

Managing sales information

In a traditional sales environment, personnel make many unsuccessful cold calls and in-person visits to customers before achieving a sale. This low rate of customer attainment is caused by the lack of organized information about customers and prospects. eCRM vendors offer software packages that manage a wide variety of leads, including information about customers, prospects, and sales forecasts, as well as other information vital to sales efforts. eCRM applications will ensure that your sales team is more informed when it enters the prospecting process.

For example, eCRM applications permit customer information requests to be turned over to sales as a potential lead for a specific product or service based on the information requested.

Fulfilling literature requests

The sales department can also automate its process by fulfilling literature requests. If a door-to-door salesperson encounters a customer who wants specific information about a product or service, the salesperson will have to go back to the office, locate the information, and deliver the information to the customer, either by mail or in person. Companies that use eCRM can automate the fulfillment of literature requests in two ways.

- Online customers can fill out an online form requesting that information be mailed to them. Although this automation saves data entry time, customers will have to wait for your inventory to be replenished if you are out of brochures, pamphlets, or other requested information.
- You can develop an online database of your literature. This allows the customer to either browse the information on your Web site or request that information be sent via e-mail. Online literature fulfillment not only provides customers with the information they need quickly, it also saves the sales department from spending time and money on printing and distributing hard copies of information.

Moreover, after mailing information to your customers once, you have the opportunity to mail more information to them. This could include special discount offers, information about other products, and electronic surveys that indicate the levels of customer interest in your products and their satisfaction with your company.

Configuring products online

You can also automate sales processes through online product configuration. For companies that offer customized products and services, an eCRM solution can save staff time and increase order efficiency by enabling individual customers and distribution partners to place customized orders online. Through an extensive database of options, customers and partners can enter the Web site and click their way through a series of customization options. The result is a customized order, placed by customers and partners.

Impact on other departments

By automating its processes, the sales department can provide valuable information to other departments within a company. For example, by automating online ordering and payments, the sales department can provide financial information about customers to the accounting department. This sharing of information decreases the number of times that information has to be entered into company records and the likelihood of data entry error.

The sales department can also generate customer and prospect information for the marketing department. By knowing exactly who is interested in your product, who is on the verge of leaving your organization due to a bad experience, and who your most valuable customers are, the marketing department can generate targeted campaigns to retain, acquire, and appeal to valuable customers.

Do it!

B-2:   Automating the sales department

Exercises

1 In the following scenario, Greg, the Customer Services manager, Benjamin, the Sales manager, and Jonathan, the Marketing manager, are sitting around a table in the conference room. As the scene starts, the meeting is about to wind up.

Greg: If no one has anything else to add, I think we're done here, guys.

Benjamin: *(looks over at Jonathan)* I'd like to add a quick thanks to you, Randy, and your marketing department. Your lead helped us land the Brownlee account.

Jonathan: *(smiles)* Really? We just sent over their request for more product information.

Benjamin: *(nods)* Yeah, well it turns out they were seriously considering changing over all their accounting software, and we convinced them to go with us. We would have never known about them if you guys hadn't passed on the info.

Greg: *(laughs and nods towards Jonathan)* It sounds like your department owes his department lunch.

In this scenario, the information that the marketing department shared with the sales department has resulted in a big sale for the company. Do you have such experience in your work life? If yes, share your experience.

2 Choose the sales processes that can be automated under the eCRM program.

A   Managing sales complaints

B   Fulfilling literature requests

C   Configuring products online

D   Tracking personnel changes

E   Managing sales information

F   Providing online customer satisfaction surveys

3 Select the advantages of fulfilling literature request online.

   A   Provides way of tracking online complaints

   B   Provides an opportunity for further e-mail contact

   C   Helps sales department reach goals faster

   D   Saves time and money on printing and distribution

   E   Provides customers with information more effectively

4 In this scenario, Benjamin, the Sales manager, is sitting across from Jonathan, the Marketing manager, who is on the phone in Jonathan's office.

   Jonathan: *(hanging up the phone)* Sorry about that, Carl. Now what can I do for you?

   Benjamin: I just wanted to come by and tell you about some things we've been hearing over in sales. Our last three new accounts said the new software's ease-of-use is what persuaded them to go ahead and buy from us.

   Jonathan: Really? We've been brainstorming ideas for our new marketing campaign and thought about promoting the ease-of-use functions. However, we weren't sure if that was a big enough selling point.

   Benjamin: *(leans forward)* Well, in addition to those other accounts, I'd say at least 75% of the purchasers mention the ease-of-use functions.

   Jonathan: *(nods)* Thanks for the heads-up, Carl. It sounds like we need to re-think certain things for the upcoming campaign.

   How does automating the sales department help the marketing department?

Automate the customer service department

Explanation

To automate the processes of the customer service department, eCRM permits companies to use the following:

- Internet self-help features
- Online product registration features
- Online customer satisfaction surveys

Internet self-help features

The customer service department can automate its processes by employing Internet self-help features for customers. In a traditional customer service department, representatives in call centers answer service calls from customers. Although this method of service works well for most companies and customers, eCRM applications permit companies to establish Internet self-help features. To implement these features, a database of information is made available to customers through the Web site of the company. Customers can access these help files 24 hours a day, seven days a week. If they need assistance after reviewing this information, they can contact the company for additional help and speak with a call center agent. These electronic help databases save customer service representatives time by assisting customers in matters they can handle themselves.

Online product registration features

The customer service department can implement an online product registration feature on your Web site. Rather than register their products over the telephone or through the mail, customers can go to the Web site of the company and fill out a product registration form. After they register, the information is entered into the company's database, and a confirmation letter with the registration information is sent in the form of e-mail to the customer.

Online customer satisfaction surveys

Your customer service department can also implement online customer satisfaction surveys. These surveys can either appear on your Web site or be sent in the form of e-mail to customers. You can use the results to identify dissatisfied customers and review their history before implementing any kind of recovery strategy. Customer satisfaction surveys can also identify features that your customers would like your company to offer. Nevertheless, you must not overwhelm or irritate customers by sending too many surveys.

Impact on other departments

Automating customer service processes can also help other departments in your company. For example, the marketing department can use online customer satisfaction surveys to identify effective marketing campaigns. This information can also be used to determine successful product features, brands, and promotional strategies.

Do it!   B-3:   Automating the customer service department

Exercises

1   Watch the movie. Discuss how the customer was able to figure out an ordering problem.

2   Have you experienced this kind of situation in your life? If yes, share your experience.

3   Choose the customer service processes that can be automated by using eCRM.

    A   Internet self-help features

    B   Online product registration features

    C   Sales information

    D   Literature request features

    E   Online customer satisfaction surveys

    F   Configuring products online

4   What are some of the advantages of offering online customer satisfaction surveys?

    A   Identify dissatisfied customers

    B   Determine successful and unsuccessful hiring practices

    C   Determine successful and unsuccessful promotional strategies

    D   Determine better pricing measures

    E   Determine new features that customers need

Automate the accounting department

You can use eCRM to automate the following processes in the accounting department:

- Pipeline management
- Online order processing

Pipeline management

Accounting can monitor various sales channels, such as direct, retail, and online sales to maintain and improve the processes. Improving pipeline management will also permit the accounting department to manage, plan, and forecast the demand for these sales channels.

Online order processing

Accounting can implement online order processing features. As a result, the accounting department will not have to process orders from customers and partnering firms. Customers and partners can place orders online, and the information used by the accounting department will automatically be recorded in the appropriate database.

Impact on other departments

Automating the accounting department also helps other departments in your company. For example, if the accounting personnel know the pipeline operations, the logistics department will be able to efficiently schedule manufacturing and production based on the information provided to them by the sales-channel analysis of the accounting department. Moreover, online order processing systems can also help other departments in terms of managing inventory, determining the available warehousing space, and reducing the likelihood of out-of-stock items and back-ordered items.

Do it!

B-4:   Automating the accounting department

Exercises

1 Choose the accounting processes that can be automated under the eCRM program.

   A   Pipeline management and online order processing

   B   Employee payroll tracking and pipeline management

   C   Online order processing and customer prospect management

   D   Sales information management and configuring online products

2 Online order processing systems can help determine the available warehousing space in your company. True or false?

Unit summary: eCRM

Topic A   In this unit, you learned about the difference between **CRM** and **eCRM**. You learned that eCRM focuses on managing **customer relationships** through the **Internet**. Next, you learned about the various features of eCRM, such as **self-service knowledge base**, **automated e-mail response**, and **customization** of **Web content**. Then, you learned about the various **disadvantages** of eCRM.

Topic B   Finally, you learned about eCRM **automation**. You learned that automating CRM helps manage customer relationships effectively. You also learned about automating the marketing, sales, customer service, and accounting departments.

Review questions

In the following scenario, Medical Supply Inc. MSI, is a company that specializes in sophisticated medical supplies. Icon International has acquired MSI to contribute to Icon's Health Care division.

Now, the company plans to incorporate MSI into their overall eCRM efforts. As the Chief Operating Officer of Icon, you need to identify the advantages, features, and disadvantages of eCRM to ensure that your team makes an informed decision. You'll also need to discuss the opportunities for automating the marketing and sales process of MSI.

1   What do you think is the advantage of incorporating MSI into the overall eCRM efforts of Icon?

2   What are the features found in successful eCRM applications?

   A   Customization of Web content

   B   Online cross-selling and volume discounts

   C   Self-service knowledge base

   D   Fast response time

   E   Unlimited public access

   F   Automated e-mail response

   G   Person-to-person contact

3   One disadvantage of implementing MSI is the inadequate feedback from customers. How do you think your company can overcome this?

4 What do you think is the first step in automating the marketing department of MSI?

5 How can you reduce the response time for customer queries?

6 How can eCRM help the ordering process?

Unit 6

eCRM customization and goals

Unit time: 45 minutes

Complete this unit, and you'll know how to:

A Customize eCRM.

B Achieve CRM goals through eCRM.

Topic A: eCRM customization

Explanation

Companies that use eCRM follow strategies that will affect every stakeholder in the organization. As a result, it is important for all who use eCRM to understand their specific roles in the process. Moreover, to remain competitive, your company must customize the eCRM marketing efforts based on customer needs.

Stakeholders that benefit from eCRM

The four main categories of stakeholders who will realize the change and benefit from eCRM include:

- Front-line employees
- Managers
- Potential customers
- Customers

Front-line employees

Front-line employees are employees who tend to have direct contact with prospects and customers, such as employees in sales, order processing, and customer service departments. In a company where many departments use eCRM on a daily basis, most of these users are front-line employees. These employees enter information into eCRM databases and recall previously entered information from databases to help manage customer relationships.

For example, a customer calls a representative in the customer service department inquiring about a payment schedule. This representative quickly recalls information about the past payment history of this customer, answers the payment question, and offers new payment terms based on the credit history of the customer.

Managers

Managers receive important information related to forecasting and trends from the report features available through eCRM. For example, suppose the marketing department needs to find out the type of customers who would be receptive to a new Internet marketing campaign. The marketing department can use the eCRM database along with the reports feature to determine the target audience for this campaign. Based on historical data, the department decides to target customers and prospects in the 20 to 30 year-old age group because they are the ones most likely to respond to an Internet campaign.

Managers can also use eCRM to evaluate the success of projects and campaigns. For example, the marketing department conducts preliminary research about the new campaign and decides to launch it. To test its effectiveness, the marketing manager can establish marketing tags into the eCRM software, which will provide the department with the results of the tagged information. These tags might include the win rate, the average time needed to close a sale, the average cost per transaction, the number of transactions per customer, the customer retention rate, or the average lifetime of customers. When established, these tags can produce reports that outline information data and statistics about the success of marketing campaigns. The department can use these reports to make sure future marketing efforts are both effective and efficient.

Potential customers

When correctly implemented, eCRM can incorporate many communication channels. By giving potential customers as many avenues for contact as possible, eCRM companies make sure that all interested parties have the opportunity to contact them. They also make certain that customers get the information they need in their preferred manner.

Customers

Companies permit customers to customize their Web site interfaces to meet their needs. This makes sure that customers are comfortable with their current forms of communication. This comfort level is an important marketing strategy because it is the only way to differentiate your product or service from your competitors'.

Another benefit is that customers can access their purchase and transaction histories. This access permits customers to improve how they do business with your company. For example, customers can check on the status of an order, look at past trends to determine how frequently to purchase, see if their purchasing trends have changed, and ensure that they are purchasing the appropriate materials and services.

Do it!   **A-1:   Identifying stakeholders that benefit from eCRM**

Exercises

1 In the following scenario, Valerie, a customer service representative, and Robin, a customer, are having a telephone conversation. Valerie is in her office looking at her computer screen.

> Robin: *(concerned)* We have already paid that bill. I don't understand why we're being charged a second time.

> Valerie: *(helpful)* Just a minute, Robin. I'm tracking down your order and payment history. Oh, here it is! It appears that you ordered and then cancelled a blue sweatshirt and then ordered a green one instead. For some reason the first order didn't get cleared out of billing.

> Robin: *(relieved)* I'm glad you figured out what happened. Can you fix it now?

> Valerie: *(smiling)* You bet! That charge is coming off as we speak, and we'll send out a new bill immediately. Is there anything else I can do for you?

How do service representatives benefit from eCRM?

2 How do managers benefit from eCRM?

A They can measure the morale of the employees.

B They can track the overtime hours in real time.

C They can evaluate the success of projects and campaigns.

D They can predict profit margins better.

E They can obtain forecasting and trend information through reports.

3 Identify the beneficial feature of each user type: front-line employees, managers, potential customers, and current customers.

Ability to obtain forecasting and trend information through eCRM reports

Ability to customize their Web site interface

Ability to enter and recall customer information from databases

Ability to obtain information in their most preferred way

Customize eCRM

Explanation

To remain competitive, your company must have the ability to communicate electronically. Competition is fierce online, so you must take advantage of every marketing opportunity that might benefit your company. Many companies that sell products and services online find it difficult to retain customers. All that customers need to do to move on to competition is type in a new Web site address. As a result, it is important for you to customize your marketing campaigns. You can customize your eCRM marketing efforts by using the following methods:

- Personalize the message
- Personalize the offer
- Personalize the communication channel

Personalize the message

Although eCRM permits you to communicate with many customers simultaneously, you can still provide customized messages. For example, you are a customer who has recently applied for a credit card through the Web site of an eCRM company. You might receive a solicitation e-mail that includes your name and information specific to your account for an electronic payment service offered through the Web site of the company.

As communication through e-mail can be impersonal, your company should make an effort to leverage personal information in e-mails to customers. Personalized solicitation messages will make your customers feel that they have established a relationship with your company, in spite of never actually having spoken to anyone.

For example, if Phil purchases a computer from your online electronics store, you should mail him a confirmation of his purchase. In that e-mail, you should include the information he provided to you in the purchase form, including his name and e-mail address, purchase information, payment agreement, warranty information, and your contact information. Personalizing the message will make your customers feel secure and satisfied when making an online purchase from your company.

Personalize the offer

You should also personalize your offers to customers by taking advantage of their explicit preferences. You can do so by allowing your customers to choose their preferences for or against products and offers. Use their implicit preferences, such as behavior history, periodicity of credit card use, typical method of payment, and ending balance to deliver relevant, personalized offers. For example, when a person applies for a credit card through the eCRM Web site, the company determines the applicant to be a new customer who has not yet made a purchase on the credit card. The customer would probably be interested in online payments or balance-protection insurance. The company might also offer a discounted interest rate for paying electronically or reward points that the customer can redeem online by conducting business over the Internet.

By personalizing offers to your customers, you let them know that you are interested in receiving their business and loyalty. You are also sending them the message that they are not mere statistics and that the company values its relationship with them.

Personalize the communication channel

Another way to personalize your marketing efforts is to use a communication channel that the customer prefers.

You can gain customer loyalty by personalizing communication channels. For example, the company determines that a customer is most receptive to e-mail communications. It sends an e-mail message to the customer informing them that e-mail can be used as the sole method of communication with the company. The credit card statements, payments, payment confirmations, inquiries, and other communications can all take place through e-mail, as opposed to other communication channels, such as telephone or mail.

Catalog retailers have found that a combination of mail and online communication about products and services is most preferred by customers. Loyal and higher transaction customers tend to use both these communication channels.

Do it!   ## A-2:   Customizing eCRM

Multiple-choice questions

1   What type of information should be used to personalize an e-mail message to an online purchaser?

   A   Information about upcoming sales

   B   Information provided in purchase form

   C   Name and e-mail address of the purchaser

   D   Hiring information

   E   Contact information of the company

2   Select the ways in which a company can customize its marketing efforts.

   A   Personalize the message

   B   Personalize the offer

   C   Personalize the price for past customers

   D   Personalize the music

   E   Personalize the look by gender

   F   Personalize the communication channel

Topic B: eCRM goals

Explanation   Although CRM and eCRM differ in their definitions, they share the same goals. Both these approaches aim at achieving supreme relationships with customers by efficiently managing customer information and using it to promote customer satisfaction.

Goals

eCRM generally has the following goals:

- Customer identification
- Data management
- Success measurement
- Analysis speed
- Return on investment

Customer identification

The first goal of implementing CRM is improving your ability to identify profitable customers. eCRM companies have a large collection of customer information in a single database. When customers communicate electronically through an eCRM Web site, the data is automatically filed in the database of the company.

When the company wants to retrieve information about profitable customers from the database, it can identify these customers and divide them into predetermined target markets. It can also generate letters and e-mails to contact them for solicitations, order confirmations, registration information, and warranty information.

Data management

CRM helps companies to manage data more efficiently. As eCRM operates in real time, it offers a faster turnaround. For example, an online purchase module of a Web site might be based on rules. When a customer orders a laptop computer, a carrier case is offered automatically. In other words, some of the eCRM analyses and insights are automatically incorporated into the online process.

Success measurement

CRM provides an accurate method for measuring success. eCRM applications help increase the effectiveness of these methods. In fact, the software generates automatic reports that are sent to affected stakeholders, outlining the status of individual projects.

Analysis speed

CRM increases the speed at which information can be processed, analyzed, and reviewed. eCRM applications increase this speed further by removing most human interactions. After customer information has been automatically entered into the eCRM database through forms, surveys, and other information entry points, the application automatically generates and disburses reports that outline the status of specific campaigns and projects.

Return on investment

eCRM programs can produce higher ROIs than traditional CRM because online integration tends to be less expensive to implement as compared to traditional channels, such as telephone, direct mail, in person, or point-of-sale channels. The value of your eCRM ROI depends on whether you base the evaluation on the cost of the entire eCRM system or on the ROI of a specific eCRM initiative or strategy. As eCRM is a new approach, it might be hard to gauge the performance of your eCRM system as compared to eCRM systems of other companies.

Evaluate the effectiveness of eCRM system

To help guarantee the success of your eCRM system, you need to evaluate it. You can ask some of these questions to evaluate the effectiveness of your eCRM system:

- Have we improved our close, or win, rate?
- Have we reduced the time needed for closing or completing a sale?
- Are we retaining more customers?
- Have we reduced the cost of closing a sale?
- Have we reduced the cost of completing a transaction?

Do it!   B-1:   Achieving CRM goals through eCRM

Exercises

1   Why is analysis speed an important goal of CRM and eCRM?

   A   It helps keep customer happier and more loyal.

   B   It enables quick reactions to changes in market conditions.

   C   It enables quick reactions to personnel changes.

   D   It helps companies to reach profitable goals quickly.

2   Medical Supply Inc. MSI, is a company that specializes in sophisticated medical supplies. Icon International has acquired MSI to contribute to Icon's Health Care division. Icon plans to incorporate MSI into their overall eCRM efforts. The company feels that this is the best way to achieve the CRM goals faster. You need to explain how eCRM helps achieve the CRM goals of Icon.

What are the ways in which eCRM helps companies to achieve CRM goals.

   A   Operates in real time

   B   Increases speed by removing most human interactions

   C   Collects customer information and integrates it into one database

   D   Tracks more complete customer information, such as employment history

   E   Needs less expense to implement than traditional channels

   F   Increases speed by increasing human interactions

   G   Splits customer information into two distinct categories

How can eCRM increase the speed at which information is processed?

eCRM programs can produce higher ROIs than traditional CRM. Give a reason to justify this statement.

Unit summary: eCRM customization and goals

Topic A   In this unit, you learned about **customizing** eCRM. You learned that to remain competitive, eCRM marketing efforts must be customized based on customer needs. Next, you learned about the various **stakeholders**, such as **front-line employees** and **managers**, who benefit from eCRM. Then, you learned that you can customize your CRM efforts by **personalizing** the **message**, **offer**, and **communication channel**.

Topic B   Finally, you learned about the **goals** of eCRM. You learned that although CRM and eCRM differ in their definitions, they share the same goals, including **customer identification**, **data management**, **success measurement**, **analysis speed**, and **return on investment**.

Review questions

1   What are the changes that the stakeholders can experience by implementing eCRM?

2   What internal changes need to be carried out when implementing eCRM?

3   How does eCRM customize customer interaction?

4   How does eCRM help CRM achieve its goal of finding and fostering relationships with profitable customers?

   A   All customer information is split between two distinct databases.

   B   It tracks only customers with the highest paying jobs.

   C   It red flags customers with the highest credit card debts.

   D   All customer information is contained in one database.

5 What are some implicit customer preferences that can help personalize customer offers?

A Frequency of credit card use

B Educational background

C Behavior history

D Health

E Employment history

F Typical payment method

Customer Relationship Management

Course summary

This summary contains information to help you bring the course to a successful conclusion. Using this information, you will be able to:

A Use the summary text to reinforce what you've learned in class.

B Determine the next courses in this series (if any), as well as any other resources that might help you continue to learn about customer relationship management.

Topic A: Course summary

Use the following summary text to reinforce what you've learned in class. It is not intended as a script, but rather as a starting point.

Customer Relationship Management

Unit 1

In this unit, you learned about the **benefits** of creating **loyal customers** and how to create loyal customers by developing **dedicated employees**, making the **services memorable**, and building **smooth relationships** with customers. Next, you learned about the **marketing tiers** that facilitate the development of customer relationships. You also learned about **MIE** and its goals.

Unit 2

You learned about the different **types** of CRM. Next, you learned about the **elements** of CRM that will help your organization become customer focused. You also learned about the four steps in the **CRM process**. Then, you learned about the **benefits** that an organization enjoys by implementing a CRM system and the **challenges** that might result in the failure of the system.

Unit 3

In this unit, you learned about the **costs** associated with CRM. You also learned about the **economic impact** of CRM implementation. Next, you learned about the **CRM implementation team** and the two types of team members, primary and secondary. You also learned about the departments that are affected by CRM and the reasons for the **failure** of a CRM program. Finally, you learned how to test a CRM program.

Unit 4

You learned how to redesign your **work processes**. Next, you learned about the factors that make it necessary to implement CRM in **stages**. Finally, you learned about the various **steps** of **CRM implementation**.

Unit 5

In this unit, you learned how to **differentiate** CRM and eCRM. You also learned about the **features** and **disadvantages**. Next, you learned about eCRM **automation**, which helps manage customer relationships effectively. Finally, you learned about automating the marketing, sales, customer service, and accounting departments.

Unit 6

You learned about **customizing** eCRM. You can customize eCRM by **personalizing** the message, offer, and communication channel. You also learned about the various **stakeholders** who benefit from eCRM. Finally, you learned about the **goals** of eCRM.

Topic B: Continued learning after class

It is impossible to learn about any subject effectively in a single day. To get the most out of this class, you should begin making use of customer relationship management techniques you've learned as soon as possible. Course Technology also offers resources for continued learning.

Next courses in this series

This is the only course in this series.

Other resources

Course Technology's partner company, NETg, offers a full line of online and computer-based courses on customer relationship management and a variety of other subjects. For more information, visit www.netg.com. This course maps precisely to the following three NETg courses:

- *Customer Relationship Management: Fundamentals of CRM*
  Course number: 44031

- *Customer Relationship Management: Implementing CRM*
  Course number: 44032

- *Customer Relationship Management: eCRM*
  Course number: 44033

Glossary

Business case

Details the process and cost of each project, such as staff, training, technology, and outsourced resources.

Corporate amnesia

Loss of customer information as a customer moves from one part of an organization to another.

Critical success factors (CSF)

Evaluation criteria that are developed before a change is implemented.

Customer relationship management (CRM)

An approach that companies use to manage customer information in a way that facilitates customer acquisition and devotion.

Customer segments

Groups of customers that share common characteristics.

Data synchronization

Ability to update and distribute information across computers that are not networked, such as laptops and other mobile machines.

eCRM

An electronic communications approach used by all stakeholders to help establish, develop, and manage relationships with customers.

Front-line employees

Employees who have direct contact with prospects and customers, such as employees in sales, order processing, and customer service departments.

Internal CSFs

Pertain to the internal operations of a business.

IT CSFs

Deal specifically with the technology parameters that the company needs.

Market intelligence enterprise (MIE)

A company that focuses on reaching the most profitable customers to obtain a competitive gain over other companies.

Marketing

Process of identifying what your customers want and developing methods to satisfy their needs.

META tags

Lists of key words you submit to search engine sites.

Pilot test project

Practice run of the CRM system to test the effectiveness of CRM within the company.

ROI ratio

The amount of money a company saves by investing compared to the amount of money spent on the investment.

Self-service knowledge base

A variety of online information sources, including help menus and links to other Web sites that guide customers through specific interactions on a Web site.

Index

U

W